WINE'S COMPANY

THE ENTERTAINING WINE COURSE

WINE'S COMPANY

A COURSE OF 20 WINE TASTING SESSIONS

PAMELA VANDYKE PRICE

W. FOULSHAM & CO. LTD.
LONDON · NEW YORK · TORONTO · CAPE TOWN · SYDNEY

W. Foulsham & Company Limited
Yeovil Road, Slough, Berkshire, SL1 4JH

ISBN 0–572–01308–6

Printed in Great Britain at
St. Edmundsbury Press, Bury St. Edmunds.

CONTENTS

Number	Theme
1	The contribution of a) dry white wines b) red wines
2	Two wines to demonstrate the style of two German regions, plus an Alsace to show how admirable the Riesling grape can be
3	Wines that are light, inexpensive and agreeable to drink with casual food can still be worthwhile, as some of them illustrate the character of unfamiliar vineyard regions and unusual grapes
4	Introducing the great grapes of Bordeaux – Cabernet Sauvignon, Sauvignon Blanc and Sémillon – and learning about the difference noble rot can make to a wine
5	A unique wine, formerly local, now known everywhere, showing the sort of wine that is needed to stand up to difficult foods
6	Learning to tell the difference between wines from cool, hot and cold, and temperate vineyards, and trying another example which demonstrates noble rot

Wines	Available from:	Page
1 Liebfraumilch Blue Nun (H. Sichel and Sons, London bottled) **2** 1980 Bulls Blood of Eger (Egri Bikavér bottled by Colman's of Norwich)	Many retail outlets	69
1 Bereich Bernkastel, Langenbach **2** Bereich Nierstein, Langenbach **3** 1981 Riesling d'Alsace Gustav Lorentz of Bergheim	Threshers; Ashe & Nephew	75
1 Austrian Grüner Veltliner **2** Italian Raboso del Veneto	Sainsbury's	80
1 Château Loudenne 1983, château bottled **2** Château Loudenne 1982 (red), château bottled **3** 1978 Château Loupiac Gaudiet, château bottled	Peter Dominic	83
Vinho Verde (branco)	Marks & Spencer	89
1 Muscadet de Sèvre et Maine **2** 1974 Dão, Regão de Marcada **3** Monbazillac	Sainsbury's	93

7	Learning how to complement rich diches with appropriate wines – here all wines from Italy
8	Some Loire wines, each from a single classic wine grape: Chenin Blanc, Sauvignon, Cabernet Franc
9	Learning more about the Chenin Blanc with some southern hemisphere wines and introducing an unusual grape, the Pinotage
10	How an unknown wine can sharpen your perception and appreciation of the classics
11	Registering black grapes from southern French vineyards
12	Introducing the Morio Muscat grape, trying a variation on the Loire Chenin Blanc, and learning to recognise the distinctive Rioja
13	Registering the Syrah grape
14	The Syrah plus the Cinsaut – an example of how modern wine-making techniques can make good small scale classics

1 Verdicchio **2** Bardolino **3** Lambrusco	Sainsbury's	98
1 Chenin Blanc, Rémy Pannier **2** Sancerre, 1983, Patient Cottat **3** Cabernet de Touraine 1982, Cuvée Prestige **4** Chateau de Breuil 1983, Coteaux du Layon	Oddbins	103
1 KWV Chenin Blanc 1982 (South Africa) **2** Houghton Supreme 1981 (Western Australia) **3** 1982 Culemborg Pinotage (Paarl, South Africa)	Waitrose	109
1 Apremont (Savoie) 1983 **2** 1983 Soave Classico, Masi **3** 1983 Moulin-à-Vent, Pasquier Desvignes **4** 1982 Brown Brothers Late Picked Muscat Blanc, Milawa Estate, Victoria	Oddbins	114
1 Grenache rosé, vin du table **2** Vin de pays de l'Uzège	Victoria Wine	119
1 Vouvray 1983 **2** Morio Muskat (Rheinpfalz) **3** 1875 Marqués de Romeral Rioja (optional)	Marks & Spencer	122
Syrah de l'Ardèche	Cullens	126
Cante Cigale Cinsault/Syrah	Waitrose	128

1 Vin de pays, Côtes de Gascogne **2** Foncalieu Cabernet Sauvignon 1982, vin de pays de l'Aude **3** Montana Marlborough Province Cabernet Sauvignon 1979, product of New Zealand	Waitrose	131
1 Dry vermouth as apéritif **2** Beaujolais Blanc (Louis Jadot) **3** Gigondas 1982 **4** Muscat de Beaumes de Venise, Domaine de Durban	Victoria Wine	136
1 Bellingham Cape Gold **2** Cuvée Latour 1982, Louis Latour **3** Côtes de Beaune Villages 1982, Delamont **4** Hautes Côtes de Nuits Villages 1979, Joseph Drouhin	Threshers; Ashe & Nephew	141
1 Gisborne 1982 Gewurztraminer, Cook's New Zealand Wine Company **2** 1982 Gewurztraminer d'Alsace, Louis Gisselbrecht **3** 1980 Torres Coroñas	Cullens	147
1 Verdicchio dei Castelli di Jesi 1983 **2** Grunberger Stein **3** Rosemount Estate Cabernet Sauvignon 1980 **4** KWV Golden Vintage 1981	Victoria Wine	151
1 1984 Old Triangle Vineyard Barossa Valley Riesling, Hill-Smith Estate, Angaston, South Australia **2** 1977 Viña Undurraga Santa Ana, Pinot Noir, Chile	Cullens	156

PREFACE

Many people have helped in the preparation of this book and, although it is possible only to name the firms concerned, it should be realised that several individuals have been involved from each. Their advice and patience in the preliminary discussions, their practical assistance with the samples and checking of information have, throughout, been of great value .

What must be stressed is that, although all the wines were available in the different outlets at the time when this book went to press, changes in vintages, sources of supply, economic trends may all have resulted in some of the wines mentioned not being exactly the same at the time of publication. No one can be blamed for this. Throughout I have done my best to indicate the sort of changes that may have affected my comments, if the wines are not identical with those I've been discussing. But wine, a living thing, cannot be static – one of the reasons why it is a perennially renewed pleasure. May the users of this book discover as much of interest and enjoyment as I have done in putting it together.

INTRODUCTION

You enjoy drinking wine. Well – you've got thus far in this book, so you must do! But do you have a feeling that perhaps you're not an 'expert', you can't easily become a 'wine taster', that 'it's all difficult and time-consuming'? Forget all this!

To start with, no one is an 'expert' in wine. Some people have more experience of wine than others and, along the way, have gained background knowledge and some ability with the practical side of selecting and serving wine. That's all that marks them out from you. Every single wine lover starts all over again with every single glass of wine they pick up. We're all beginners. Beware anybody who introduces themselves as an 'expert', 'connoisseur', 'wine buff' – that's the type who is likely to be the wine snob, whose opinions are unlikely to be of interest and whose company is not sought by those who really do know something. Those worthwhile people, incidentally, are far more likely to be interested in *you* – why you like certain wines and don't care so much for others. They are the wine lovers who go on drinking and learning literally until the last glass – in whose company wine is fun, stimulating and fascinating. As regards being a 'wine taster' – do you think of anyone who is a good cook as a 'food eater'? And how can you appraise any wine without tasting it? If you drink with discrimination and think about what you drink, whether you like it or not, then you're tasting. It's that simple.

GOOD WINE DOESN'T

HAVE TO BE EXPENSIVE

No one can ever know everything about wine – that's why sometimes it may seem a difficult study. But that's also why the beginner has a contribution to make, side by side with the world-famous authority. Of course it can take time. So it does to become familiar with anything worthwhile – you can fall in love in an instant, but knowledge only comes with study and perseverance. This needn't be dull – that's the good thing about wine – and it needn't be expensive, either. People often suppose that only the great and costly wines are the preferred drinks of those who can afford them and who are well-known in the world of wine. Not so. These are treats, for special occasions. To find a cheap wine that is thoroughly enjoyable, to discover an unfamiliar wine that contributes the attributes of its region, maybe of a local grape and a previously unknown wine maker, all this is exciting and rewarding in terms of liquid pleasure. And behind the cheap wines there are some great authorities – for, whereas someone with a big bank balance can buy the 'big stuff' when it's available, it takes real know-how to select, maybe from several hundred samples, the sort of wine that *you* can afford to buy several times a month from the high street – and that you will enjoy so much that you'll come back for more. Wine of this kind can be very big business. The very finest wines of the world are usually in short supply and they are not the money makers, because it costs so much to make them anyway. It's the 'bread and butter' lines that can make the profits – because they are sold (if successful and liked by the public) in such huge quantities.

Why not just drink?

There is a slight difference between drinking wine and tasting it. The experience of tasting is critical – you are trying to work out why you like – or, even, why you don't like – this particular wine in your glass. You may find it similar to other wines you've enjoyed, or perhaps you are interested in associating it with places you've visited in vineyard regions – tasting it may make it complete previous experiences. For example, if you have been to Italy and visited the Chianti countryside in Tuscany, you may discover a wine akin to those you enjoyed while on holiday, but there's a difference: now, is this difference the result of the wine coming from a different region within the Chianti vineyard – so you should try to find the wine you originally sampled again – or is the wine older, from another producer, or is it simply that you've developed a preference for a drier or a sweeter style of wine? Tasting can assist your shopping, by guiding you to the wines you'll probably like and steering you away from those you may not care for so much.

Of course, the purpose of wine is to give you enjoyment when you drink it. But suppose it doesn't? Do you always know why? Maybe it's because you've rushed home with the bottle, pulled the cork – and possibly served it with something that dulls its flavour? Or is the wine truly defective – and should be taken back to the shop? Or, again, is this an instance of a particular wine not being a wine 'for you'? No one can like every single wine, not even the greatest. Indeed, it's a good thing we don't like all the same wines, because, if we did, there would only need to be three vats, red, white and pink, in the world – and all the fun of trying, discovering, discussing, arguing and generally exploring would be lost.

Tasting wine is a bit like assisting at the rehearsal of a play or concert, or watching someone work out at a sport. For the seriously interested, this can be of great interest, you see how certain things happen and why. With wine it isn't difficult if you have a fellow-enthusiast to share the experience (for wine is always more enjoyable when shared). It does help, though, to have some points to watch for, which is where this book aims to assist.

If you simply like drinking, go ahead. But if you'd like to know a bit more about the wines it is suggested you drink, this is a guide as you begin. It *will not* enable you to 'know the difference in a blind tasting between one wine and another'! People who can do this are very clever – it can, however, be easy for a tasting to fool even the most experienced. Anyone can go wrong – and nobody should mind when they do so; they may not be 'on their day', they may have had something that distracts or influences them, they may have had a piece of chocolate half an hour beforehand (see p. 171 for what *that* can do to the palate) or they may unwisely have assumed that they are going to taste one sort of wine, when in fact something quite different is in the glass! Indeed, sometimes the more you know, the more mistakes you can make when tasting blind, simply because you risk being confused by all the information you've acquired.

None of this makes you better or worse – as long as you're not taking part in a competition or an exam. But tasting a wine can alert you to it, so that you find it more interesting than if you merely drank it. Also – the wine goes into you, becomes part of you. Shouldn't you be interested in it?

Social Wine Tasting

Wine is much talked about today and even the most modest bottle can arouse comment and discussion. In addition, though you'd certainly not criticise someone's choice of food to their face, especially if they'd cooked it, you can cheerfully argue about the particular wine selected for an occasion without giving offence. It's helpful if you can make constructive suggestions – mentioning wines you've recently discovered, something you drank at a study session, why you consider X & Co.'s 'house red' to be better than the 'house red' of Z & Co., or that Firm Such-and-Such has given a tasting at which their sparkling wine was outstanding value.

Finally, there are the advantages. Knowing even the basics of tasting make you an appreciated guest and host whose invitations are prized – 'Always something special to drink' – and you're unlikely to feel hesitation even when faced with a poster-sized wine list in a luxury restaurant. But just that little extra knowhow can add enormously to your private enjoyment, even the bottle that accompanies beans on toast. So – try tasting and you'll find the experience offers far more fun than you could have expected.

HOW TO USE THIS BOOK

With all the wines available, it's often difficult to make a choice.

To help you range around the bottles, selecting some wines for particular occasions, this book contains some basic guidelines giving a series of tasting sessions. These will help you with the 'props' – glasses, opening bottles, budgeting and estimating quantities, but, most importantly, they suggest how you can both taste seriously, which isn't a solemn matter, and also enjoy the wines you taste with suitable food.

The book is intended as a wine course using wines from high street retail outlets. You don't have to follow the course through from session I to the end, you can pick and choose the sessions as you please, as each has a particular theme. Choose the session you want to use, go out and buy the wines you are going to try with or without friends, then look under **Practicalities** for instructions on what to do with the wines to prepare them for tasting. When you are ready to taste, read through **What you are aiming to do** and then start to taste using the **Tasting Notes** to help you as you go.

The wines selected for the tasting sessions are mostly widely available, either as nationally-distributed brands, or through the sort of retail outlets likely to be easy of access to many people. Of course, if you do live somewhere remote, you may not be able to find them, but there are some suggestions for certain special occasions that can be ordered from wine merchants, in addition to supermarkets and retail chains. Otherwise, all the bottles are in the medium to slightly special range, some being definitely cheap.

What can't be done is to recommend specific fine wines, including those that vary considerably from year to year – because, in certain areas, the wine of, say, 1982 may be very different (better or less good) than the wine of 1983 and any tasting notes will consequently be different too. But, as the bulk of all wine is non-vintage, you still have plenty to choose from and, with the more special wines, there's guidance as to the overall style of them so you don't risk, for example, getting a very dry, rather hard wine when what you'd prefer is something rather softer although not necessarily sweet.

Because what you eat affects what you drink – and vice versa – the sorts of foods that partner certain wines are indicated. You'll find notes on foods that definitely fight with wine, also dishes that make most wines taste extra-good. The menu suggestions are deliberately everyday and even occasionally humble. Always remember that wine is *the* supreme convenience food – if someone drops in when you've only got cheese and fresh fruit or simply lingers so that they have to be asked to 'take pot luck' and you 'stretch' the fish pie by opening a can or frozen vegetable pack, then it's the bottle that can make the meal not only more enjoyable as an occasion, but the food taste better.

General procedure for the tasting sessions

The general plan is to suggest two or more bottles (you can always finish up the wine you don't drink the day after) to taste. It's not easy to taste a single wine at a time; the contrast or similarity of another wine – or wines – makes it easier for you to form clear impressions. So you and your friend, husband, wife, colleague or group of enthusiasts taste the wines with the aid of the practical advice given (pp. 62–68) plus the detailed comments on the particular wines that I've provided after also tasting them in company. You don't have to agree with these tasting notes, but some of the information may give you a starting point so that you can then go on tasting and voicing your own opinions.

Then there are suggestions as to the sort of food you might serve after the tasting session, with which you can drink the wines. Naturally, you needn't follow these slavishly, but you'll find advice about the overall type of recipe that can go well with the particular bottles. If you're an ambitious cook, you can show off with the menu; if not, you can go for bread, cheese and fruit on some occasions, or fall back on a reliable stew or even a trusted take-away dish.

Remember always – wine is to be enjoyed. So, if you're sharing one of these occasions with several people, make it a happy occasion. Don't be solemn – the laughter around many of the tables presided over by the world's greatest wine makers is as precious and memorable as the priceless liquid in the glasses. Make it clear that you want people to be interested –

their comments are as valuable as your opinions. Show them some of the very simple devices that make wine taste better – let them sample a wine from a glass you've kept upended on a sheet of plastic side by side with one kept upright in the air: they are unlikely to opt for the plasticised glass! Show them how a sparkling wine soon goes flat in a 'saucer' glass, or how it's much easier to get the bouquet of a wine from a tulip or goblet glass than from a tumbler – and they'll enjoy drinking from the right shape of glass from then on. It's sad when people think wine is 'difficult' – but once get them involved with 'doing it themselves' and they'll not only find how easy it is to enjoy and sample, before long they'll be telling you things you didn't know! No one can know everything, which is why those of us who love wine are always greedy about picking the brains of others who love it too.

If you find that any of the advice or suggestions in this book don't suit you, then don't force yourself to try and follow them. Do your own thing – there are as many ways of appreciating and studying wine as there are colours in a rainbow. Never try too hard – if you don't want to taste for more than fifteen minutes, don't. Don't be influenced too much by what even the most respected writers and teachers say – try to make up your own mind. Even much-publicised comments on certain wines, or detailed reports by 'panels' of tasters of various qualifications or merely diverse enthusiasm cannot substitute for what *you* think, what *you* like. Of course, such reports are interesting – but if you don't agree with them, don't think that you are in any way 'wrong'; it's always worth studying what someone more experienced has to say about a subject in which they've specialised and that you are investigating, but food and drink are extremely personal things and your views are equally important to you, so formulate them. Don't be afraid to change your mind – you're unlikely to keep to the same set of preferences in food and drink (or clothes, music, art, decoration) for the whole of your life; indeed, if you do, this may indicate that you're rather too set in your ways!

What about me? I'm hoping to guide you, in the pages of this book, through some experiences in tasting, drinking and enjoying wine. Some of the wines I like better than others but I haven't included any I don't like and the same goes for food. (If your favourite dish is omitted, that's probably why.) As

I've been studying wine for some years, it's inevitable that I know some of the facts and background of the wines I'm encouraging you to taste and, because my job is to express my impressions in words, I may be able to describe these wines in more detail and with a greater choice of words than you'll immediately be able to do. That's the only thing that makes us different. If you suddenly decide that the description of a particular wine isn't accurate as far as that wine and you are concerned and if you then make up your own description – that's exactly what I hope you'll do: go on and do it yourself. Remember, when I first started to learn about wine, I had nothing to go on but my own interest – no tradition of wine drinking in the family, no possibility of buying fine bottles frequently; I was interested and many people encouraged and taught me. If I can pass on even a fraction of the enjoyment that wine has given me to you, then this is a great reward.

DEFINITIONS

It's not difficult to sort out the different categories of drinks when you're shopping. Refer to the section on 'Labels' for details of what may be on the label of any bottle. The following apply to items you may see in shops in the UK.

Wine: The definition of this, according to The Wine & Spirit Association of Great Britain is 'The alcoholic beverage obtained from the juice of freshly gathered grapes, the fermentation of which has been carried through in the district of origin and according to local tradition and practice.'

English wine is made from grapes grown in England (there are now a few vineyards in commercial production also in Wales), crushed and fermented in this country. **British wine** is made by using dried grapes or concentrated grape juice and is produced by several reputable manufacturers and also some English vineyards. **Country wines** are made from fruits, berries, plants other than grapes and are increasingly available, some of them from installations also making English wine.

Made wine is an alcoholic beverage made by means of wine making kits, using various wine yeasts. Although 'home wine making' is a popular activity and can provide enjoyment and interest it is not and cannot be the same as wine made from freshly gathered grapes.

Fortified wine is one that is fortified, i.e. 'made stronger' by the addition of spirit, usually brandy. Port, sherry and Madeira are the best known examples.

Alcoholic strength is now usually referred to as percentage of alcohol by volume or 'Gay Lussac' after the French chemist who evolved it. It is usually easier to understand than 'proof', especially as the UK and US systems of proof are different. But the main wines fall into three categories, HM Customs & Excise levying duty on them according to their alcoholic strength:

All table wines – still, sparkling, red, white, rosé	7–14.5% alcohol by volume
Fortified wines	17–21% alcohol by volume
Vermouth and wine-based apéritifs	16–20% alcohol by volume

You cannot assess alcoholic strength merely by tasting but you don't need to – the Customs see to it that there is no risk of a high strength wine getting into a bottle of a wine you're going to enjoy with a meal. Regulations governing the production and labelling of wine vary, from region to region, country to country and, of course, there are special regulations within the EEC overall. Wines you see on sale in the UK will have had to comply with these regulations but, if you're travelling abroad, you may find the same wines labelled differently, because the same regulations may not apply. For example, in the US or Australia a sparkling wine may be referred to as 'Champagne' which would be contrary to regulations in the EEC. The use of certain names, such as 'Chablis', 'Sauternes', 'Burgundy' may likewise be seen by travellers – but it's fair to say that the use of these classic wine names is now being dropped by many producers; the wines seldom bear more than a very vague likeness to the classics anyway.

LABELS AND HOW TO INTERPRET
THEM

Every wine label and, in addition, the type of bottle, and in certain circumstances the lettering (if any) on the cork and the capsule is subject to controls. Usually, the finer the wine, the stricter these are. Wines that are bottled in the country of their origin or at the estate where they have been made are therefore subject to old-established traditions – such as the shape of the bottle and the colour of its glass – and current regulations. Wines that are shipped in bulk and bottled in the UK are not always subject to the same sort of regulations, but, in the customer's interests, traditions are maintained; you are unlikely to find a claret in a tall green bottle of the type used for Mosel, for example!

Because litre and large sizes of bottle are increasingly popular, many inexpensive wines are put up in these containers, also, of course, in the 'bags in box' packs now on the increase. Much thought is expended on the design of such labels and packs, because these are the wines that sell in vast quantities and, the shippers hope, will make a profit, whereas there is never enough very fine wine to go round. The big money is made in the 'everyday' lines, which enable the finer wines to be maintained in stock. Beware of the very fancy label – a visit to a French supermarket will show many examples of pseudo-parchment labels, 'olde' script, even mock handwriting, with pictures of medieval scenes, roistering kings and cardinals and possibly a back label recounting some picturesque legend associated with the wine. The beverage may be acceptable – it's not likely to be much more.

Regulations governing wine are continually changing, so that it's risky to generalise too much at one time. Here are a few practicalities.

Bottle sizes

It's not always easy to tell the size of a bottle – some of the plump, squat ones look smaller than the tall thin ones. The fluid contents will, however, be stated on the label – unless you find a bottle pre–1980, when this wasn't the rule. The 'average' standard wine bottle contains 75 fl. oz., but of course if you allow for the cork and a little 'ullage' (the amount of air between the top of the wine and the bottom of the cork), the actual contents may be less. Bottles of 73 cl. and 70 cl. are also in use and, with half bottles, the fluid contents will be half that of the bottle, although actually a little less because of the cork and the ullage. The difference in portioning out the wine in a 75 cl. bottle and that of a 70 cl. bottle is very little – it might be about that of the small amount poured for a tasting sample – but the overall price can be appreciably different, so, if you see a possible 'bargain' check the bottle size. The duty charged on wine is calculated on the wine in a carton of twelve bottles, so obviously there is a difference between twelve bottles of 70 cl. and twelve of 75 cl. and this affects the per bottle price.

Bottles sealed only with a small plastic stopper and covered by a metal capsule can be filled almost to the stopper, so there is less ullage, but this type of container is used only for cheap wines, likely to be used up at a session for a party. Litre bottles are increasingly in use, so are those holding 1.5 litres and even 2 litres. Many flasks of Chianti hold a litre or a half litre – if you want a bottle, then you'll get 25 cl. more than you bargained for unless you check the size of the flask! Boxed wines come in various litre sizes, the 'bag' type being of 3 litres now, the 'Tetrabrick' types of container, which enables a pack of wine to be available in the same format as a carton of juice or milk, are smaller, so are canned wines.

Types of labels

Most bottles have a main label and this can provide all the essential and required information. But there may also be a neck label, which can state the vintage, if any, possibly the name or monogram of the producer or shipper and, maybe, a recommendation to serve the wine, for example, 'frais' (cool) with certain foods. If the name of the shipper or merchant is not on the main label, it may be on a strip label, under the main label. A back label, giving more information, can be on the other side of the bottle. All these labels are subject to beady-eyed inspection by the authorities, as is the name of the wine. It's not allowed, for example, to show an individual and distinctive château or schloss on a label and call the wine 'Château (or 'Clos') Sanfairyann' or 'Schloss Frankenstein' unless there really *is* such a place and the wine has been made at the particular estate. Bottles of Champagne are not allowed to bear descriptions such as 'Près Reims' or 'Côte des Blancs', even if the producer's establishment is there – only the address may be given. Fancy bottle shapes can sometimes be used, but the colour of the glass and, for most classic wines, the bottle shape itself are in accordance with traditions. The square-shouldered bottle, usually associated with Bordeaux, is used for many wines that may throw a deposit, because the shoulder of the bottle will hold this back when the wine is poured. Bottles of dark-toned glass are used for wines that may be laid down for long-term maturation and need shielding from the light, such as vintage port, red Burgundy and Bordeaux. Green, of various tones, is used for most white wines, but brown is used for Rhine wines. Nowadays traditions are often still followed even though the original reason for the shape and colour of the bottle no longer applies. A bottle of wine should also have somewhere on its label the information as to where it was bottled – either in the country of its origin or by the shipper in the UK who imported it in bulk and bottled it here. This is a fairly recent regulation so if you find any very old bottles, the information may not be given. But the finest wines nowadays are usually bottled at the estate where they were made. What about other label terms?

Sometimes there are some comic notions as to the meanings of 'A.C.', 'D.O.C.' and so on, but they aren't difficult to understand. It's perhaps tiresome that there's no one overall international authority controlling labelling, but any reputable producer, shipper, merchant will provide adequate information about any particular wine and this is usually on the label. The thing to beware of is the totally unknown name – of a grower or a firm – no adequate address as to where they are and a suspiciously low price! It's not common for some unscrupulous person to print imaginary labels that sound very fine and slap them onto bottles of ordinary 'plonk', and fortunately such practices are usually detected and stopped; but the ordinary customer should buy wine from a reliable retailer and, if possible, try to learn even a little about what is a fair price and a correct label. After all, if someone offered you a 'diamond' ring for £5 or a 'cashmere' sweater for £1, wouldn't you query the deal?

French wines

Appellation d'Origine Contrôlée/A.O.C./A.C.: All the finer French wines are wines of appellation, although you won't see the words or initials on a bottle of Champagne, because it's the only wine not required to state this – and is very strictly controlled anyway. The A.O.C regulations stipulate where the wine comes from, the vines, how they were trained, how the wine was made, the minimum degree of alcohol in the finished wine. Each region has its own set of A.C.s, and often these fit inside each other, becoming more specific, such as, in Bordeaux, the wines may be A.C. Bordeaux, Bordeaux Supérieur and then belong to one of the particular regions, such as St. Émilion, or St. Julien. The same applies in Burgundy – the more specific the A.C., the stricter the controls on the wine – and elsewhere.

Vins Délimités de Qualité Supérieure/V.D.Q.S.: These wines must bear on the label or on a separate seal the sign of their category. They are controlled as to regions, but not quite as strictly as the A.O.C. wines. **Vins de pays/Vins de table:** this newish category of French wines means wines coming from specified regions, often with attractive-sounding names. They are often very good value. The Vins de Table are actually a slightly lower category, but a Vin de Pays may also bear the words Vin de Table on its label.

Vins de consommation courant: These are branded wines, such as you often see advertised – e.g. 'Vins du Postillon' – and are the lowest category, though usually providing pleasant drinking.

German wines

These are the labels that tend to bewilder buyers! In fact they give most detailed information. Keep calm, split up any long words into syllables and, ideally, try to consult some detailed book on German wines if you want to know more. But these are the essentials – and very easy to understand. **Tafelwein** can be a blend, including wine from EEC countries other than Germany.

Deutscher Tafelwein must come only from Germany, from one of five specified regions and from authorised grapes. The newish category of **Deutscher Landwein**, slightly higher in category than Deutscher Tafelwein, is about the same as the French Vin de Pays.

QbA wines: These are quality wines from approved grapes from eleven specified regions of Germany. Sometimes they may bear the names of particular vineyards, even of specific sites within these vineyards. Liebfraumilch comes into the QbA category, the grapes for it must come only from the Nahe, Rheinhessen or Rheinpfalz.

QmP wines: These are the 'Quality wines with a special asset or attribute', at the top of the scale. The first rung of this is the **Kabinett** wines – the term means they are special. Then there are the **Spätlese** wines, from late-picked grapes, therefore finer than average. **Auslese** wines are made from late-picked grapes that have been gone over to select only the ripest clusters. **Beerenauslese** wines, late-picked, are made from grapes selected literally grape by ripe grape. **Trockenbeerenauslese** wines are made from grapes that have been allowed to dry and shrivel on the vine ('trocken' means dry) so that each grape contains only a drop of concentrated juice. **Eiswein** is made from grapes actually frozen when they are rushed to the press long after the normal vintage. QmP wines are never cheap, but the wines of certain growers are so fine that, even in somewhat indifferent vintages, they can command high prices.

A German wine label will give: the vintage; the region; the place. With the finer wines, the specific vineyard will be named and, also, the grape. The producer's name or that of the shipper – these can look intimidatingly long – are also important, but remember that one of the longest words of all, 'Winzergenossenschaft', only means 'growers' co-operative'. The **'A.P.'** number refers to the approval of the relevant authority who has passed the wine for sale with the various terms and descriptions.

Italian wines

The initials **D.O.C.**, which stand for Denominazione di Origine Controllata and are usually abbreviated in speech to 'DOC', apply to Italian-bottled wines. The category is awarded in a slightly different way from the French A.O.C. to wines produced in accordance with tradition and approved grapes, region and methods of making. As it takes some time to award this to the numerous Italian wines, some of even the famous ones may not yet bear it on their labels. The superior classification, Denominazione di Origine Controllata e Guarantita (**D.O.C.G.**), applies to some of the finer Italian wines.

Other countries

In Spain, the various regional controls are exerted on wines, and labels specifying the wine's provenance are to be seen, including such areas as Rioja, Penedés, La Mancha, Valdepeñas, Navarra, Jumilla, Alicante, Almansa. Details of grapes, cultivation and the making of the wine are subject to the award of these labels. It should be remembered, however, that many agreeable Spanish wines may not bear the 'Denominacion di Origen' on their labels. The term **'Reserva'** implies a wine of superior quality, the terms **'Vino de mesa'** and **'Vino de pasta'** mean that the wine is a table wine in the 'everyday' price ranges. In Portugal, controls apply to port wine, vinho verde and Dão wines, these wines bearing a paper seal under the capsule, indicating their origin. Other areas, in both Spain and Portugal, will be subject to more defined controls in due course.

Overall, the important thing to bear in mind is that an indication on a wine's label as to where it comes from is important, so that you know in general what it may be like. Other information is useful – the style of wine made by one estate or one shipper or handled by one grower may appeal to one person, that characteristic of another firm be liked by another. A vintage is useful (see pp. 50–51) to indicate whether a wine is old or young, although most everyday wines are non-vintage and ready to enjoy when they are put on sale. If a label tells you that the wine should be served cool or that it may be especially pleasant served with meat or with game, this is also helpful. But remember that a wine may be completely 'correct', made and labelled exactly as it should be in accordance with regulations – and yet this can only *imply* the quality. The quality of a wine can only be the responsibility of the maker – the grower – and the shipper or merchant, who buys it and then offers it for sale to you, the paying customer. This is why the reputation of a firm, an estate, a shipper is so important – no piece of paper can *guarantee* quality, only the people involved with the wine at each stage of its development. In the same way, a wine can have a great reputation, can have been offered to you by a respected wine merchant – and even be somewhat expensive – but all the same none of this can definitely ensure that you're going to love this wine more than any other! It's possible to admire a wine without thoroughly enjoying it, but this is where, until experience can guide you, it's wise to have some advice from a wine merchant, somebody who has some knowledge of wine and, even, a writer about wine!

P A R T 1

ARRANGING YOUR

TASTING SESSIONS

There are many different ways of organising what may be termed a 'tasting'. Some people arrange what is virtually a wine and cheese party, others get a speaker to conduct a 'tutored tasting', commenting in detail on a series of wines one by one. But for the purposes of our particular sessions, I'm assuming that you are holding a short tasting session in your own home, afterwards going on to drink the few wines tasted with a suitable meal. You will probably get the chance, if you regularly buy wine, to attend the sort of tasting when a big range of wines or young wines are on show, but, for most of us, it's more practical in our homes to taste the wines we're going to drink with food slightly seriously before we actually do drink them.

In the following sessions, there are two or more wines suggested for each. This is because it's always easier to form ideas about a wine when you compare one with another. It's also much easier to taste in company, exchanging opinions. How many people are involved is, of course, up to you. Two people are a start. For more, then you must consider whether you have enough wine to go round! (For quantities to provide at tastings and at meals, see p. 50.) You may simply decide to open a couple of bottles with one other person without previous planning, or suggest to a colleague that he or she should join you for an evening or at a weekend to share a meal that will be prefaced by an appraisal of a few possibly interesting wines. Or, for special occasions, you can definitely plan a 'wine dinner', mentioning when you invite your guests that you'll be trying the wines beforehand, if any of them wish to come a little earlier and take part in the tasting. Don't, ever, make it seem that you're going to be too serious about any of this – you're merely offering friends an interesting spell of something that's an extension of your hospitality.

Organising sessions

If a friend or group of friends share your interest in wine, then it's easy to share the arrangements for these sessions as well. This doesn't just mean splitting the cost between you (although that's a help) but allocating the chores. If you plan to try several wines, then people can make themselves individually responsible for researching the background of one wine each. You'll find that, once you have got into the way of arranging these simple tasting-cum-dining sessions, you'll probably have one friend offering to 'present a bottle' that they've found of special note or value, and be willing to talk about it and, even if they don't suggest the food to serve alongside, to slot it in to any proposed selection of other wines you may wish to share with friends.

One warning here – somebody should always programme the choice of the wines. Otherwise, if you leave it to people to select something and simply bring the bottle of their choice, you may find you've got a badly balanced assortment: two sweet wines and a rather tough, gutsy red, for example, when the food is on the light side. But this 'everyone bring a bottle' can be an excellent way of comparing wines of the same sort. Suppose you announce that you propose a seafood supper and ask three or four people each to bring a bottle of Muscadet. They must be able to tell the price and the source of supply, of course. This can alert you to a retailer you may not have tried before, when you discover a pleasant wine from this source. Don't let people get the idea they must bring something expensive – stress that it's the wines all of you can afford that are interesting; the 'find' of a pleasant 'cheapie' is a real treasure.

Timing

You're unlikely to want to be popping in and out of the kitchen while you are looking at the wines (a bit of wine language is that one 'looks at' wines, which means tasting them). So don't prepare the sort of food that needs a lot of last-minute attention.

If you allow about the same sort of time for your tasting as you would for drinks before a meal anyway, then this is reasonable, but if you have more than three wines, you may need a little longer to spend over trying them.

Warning

If people really must smoke or opt out of any tasting so as to have a spirit-based drink, or if they merely come smelling deliciously of expensive scent or after-shave, then the tasters are somewhat handicapped! And if a guest brings you a gorgeously scented bouquet, you can't leave it outside until you've finished tasting. But take this in your stride – if at all possible, get the fragrant people and their drinks or flowers to stand or sit a little away from those of you who are tackling the wines. As exactly the same hazard occurs if delectable cooking smells waft in from the kitchen, you simply have to try and cope with the problem without making anyone feel they've dropped a brick. Perhaps, if you select a session of rather special wines, you can mention this in advance as a tactful warning – people are usually quite happy to fall in with such arrangements. (See **Enemies to wine** pp. 170.)

Additional Information

It's a good idea to have some reference book available, in case there's a query about exactly where a wine comes from or anything special about it. Here, you have the basic information about each wine suggested. If you want to know more, or find out the names of wines like them, or something about the country, the method of making it or anything similar, then you should have some form of general wine book, preferably with maps. There are a number of books of this kind, not all of them expensive (see pp. 191). If you are considering choosing one, then, if you can, check on the experience and qualifications of the writer or editor, also when the book was written – information that was correct ten years ago may be misleading today. And don't be beguiled by too many pretty pictures – sound text is likely to be more use to you.

Making notes

If you like, put the names of the wines you're going to taste on a piece of paper, together with the price and source of supply, and hand a copy to each guest, so that they can make notes. Otherwise, of course, you can simply read the labels.

What about palate cleansers?

If you usually serve some form of 'nibbles', go ahead. But it is an idea to steer clear of anything very piquant until you've first tried the wines. Biscuits, crisps, mild cheese 'dips' and scraps of pâté on crispbread are all unobtrusive refreshments at this stage. Keep the olives, stuffed eggs and curry puffs for a bit later, so that you can sample the wines at their best.

Do you spit?

Obviously not on the floor! Of course, at a professional tasting, with a number of wines to sample, it is necessary to spit out the tastings, and often the wines may not be ready to drink anyway. But in your home, you are drinking. The wines are ready to drink and enjoy and you don't risk taking too many at a time. True, some of us find that we do get a more critical and clear impression of some wines if we can spit out after tasting, but I don't think anyone is likely to wish to do so with the selection suggested here. (If somebody really dislikes a wine so much that they long to spit it out, then show them the bathroom.)

The surroundings

For the actual tasting it is a good idea to put a white tablecloth on the table and have a good source of light (not candles) as this is important when your guests are looking at the colour of the wines. After the tasting is over you can light the candles or dim the lights for the meal itself.

USING OTHER WINES

There are some suggestions throughout the tasting sessions giving help to anyone who cannot get hold of the same bottle as that being used. Do bear in mind that the tasting notes may not apply exactly. Also, if you do get the same wine but the vintage has changed, don't expect a very great difference in the bottles. For the purposes of this book I've selected wines that do not usually vary very much from one vintage to another.

Sometimes this is because the climate of the vineyard doesn't vary much from one year to another, sometimes it's because, with both a vintage and a non-vintage wine, the popularity of this particular wine is such that buyers want it to remain fairly constant in style, so the maker will see that there's no radical change. But be prepared for *some* variations.

Vermouth

You'll see that this is included in one of the sessions. It's one of the most useful wines you can buy, because not only can it be delicious as an apéritif or between-times drink, but it's invaluable in the kitchen. This is no place to deal with cooking with wine, but vermouth, because of the herbs and spices involved with its manufacture, is wonderful for adding to sauces, stuffings, pâtés and stock or water in which you're poaching fish or meat, or simply for providing an extra 'something' by way of flavour to many recipes.

Sherry, port, Madeira

As has been mentioned, these don't form part of the tasting sessions. But you may well keep them in your drinks cupboard or on the sideboard. If you wish to offer a glass of sweet sherry, dessert Madeira or port at the end of the meal, go ahead. But, if you offer a sherry before one of the tasting sessions you may find it difficult to appraise the wines immediately after this – because, simply on account of its higher alcoholic strength, the sherry may overpower the wine coming after it. Also, if you like a 'medium' or not too dry sherry before a meal, you may discover that a very dry table wine will taste sharp and bitter if served directly after the sherry. Bear this in mind. You have provided interesting drinks by way of wine – there's no need to serve anything else on these occasions.

Spirits

These are not included in this book – the subject is vast. If anyone wants a spirit drink before a meal, perhaps they've had a hard day and want a real reviver, then they must accept that they won't get much detailed pleasure from any table wine taken directly after this. After the end of the meal, if you are serving chocolates with coffee, then this is a possible time for your favourite spirit drink, if you want to serve it.

It's an odd but acknowledged thing that, if you can serve more than one wine at a time, the two wines always both seem better than if you sample one by itself. Suppose you have a rather special second wine – then it should have something by way of 'introduction'; the palate will thus be prepared for the special wine and, often unexpectedly, the wine that, as it were, heralds its arrival usually seems much better too. Sometimes it's of interest to compare two wines side by side – maybe they are made from the same classic wine grape but come from totally different vineyards; maybe one is much older than the other. The contrast is usually interesting and illuminating.

There's another practical reason: it's known that some people find certain wines don't agree with them, or they may not like them. There's the curious 'redhead' reaction, when even a small glass of a red wine can so upset the drinker that he develops a headache, nausea, giddiness and feels truly unwell. Others find that a very dry white wine can cause them cramps and rheumatic pains. So to have more than a single wine on a social occasion is usually wise and considerate.

Why more than two wines?

This is somewhat for the special occasion, but, if you offer one wine as an apéritif, you can then have another with the first course and the third with the main dish. Or, using one wine for apéritif and also with the first course – unless this is the sort of food (see p. 171) that doesn't require any wine by way of accompaniment – then you have a wine for the main dish of the meal plus the third to partner a pudding or cheese and fruit.

Why more than three wines?

This is party planning – whether you're going to sit round a table or invite friends to a buffet. It can be delightful to sit and compare wines with a good meal – you'll see how your own views about each wine may be slightly changed by what you are eating. And, when people can help themselves to a range of drinks, likewise a variety of different foods, such as salads and cheeses, they enjoy talking about them and comparing notes.

General order

If you are making your own selections of wines at any time, try to observe the few basic conventions: dry before sweet, young before old. A dry wine can taste bitter after a sweet one, a small-scale young wine may be disappointing if tasted after something mature and impressive. In addition, it's wise to taste cheapish wines before expensive ones, although you needn't bother about this if the wines are all within the same price range. Finally – and it concerns the final wine – try always to have the best or most enjoyable wine last, so that you end your entertainment on a high note.

WHAT ABOUT THE FOOD?

At the end of each tasting session there are suggestions for a menu that is easy to serve and prepare, to accompany the wines when you get down to drinking them. You needn't keep rigidly to this, of course, but don't try too hard to serve very elaborate meals; let the wines be the supreme 'convenience food' that they are and do the main work for you. Indeed, rather simple food, made with the best ingredients is usually the ideal accompaniment to fine wine. Good bread, good butter, good cheese, plus the appropriate bottle is something you can invite anyone to share without hesitation. Cold cuts and baked potatoes, some form of snack on toast, fresh fruit and indeed many of the popular 'take away' dishes can be served on these occasions. You'll notice that, in many wine producing countries, the cheese is served before anything sweet. This is because most wine, white as well as red, goes very well with most cheese and so the wine can be finished before the sweet course; after you've had a very sweet or creamy pudding or ice or liqueur-enriched dish, you'll find it difficult to taste any wine that may have been excellent with meat or fish, so that, unless you have a special sweet wine for the sweet course, to serve the cheese after the sweet can put any remaining 'main course' wine at a disadvantage. But this is up to you and your guests to decide.

Recipes are not given – you'll probably have your own cookery books to work from or have your own favourite dishes. Check with the 'Enemies to wine' section (pp. 170) when you plan an original menu. Otherwise, if in any doubt, keep the food simple. I know that a cook proud of his or her skill often wants to show off with a particular recipe, or else offer a selection of sweet things at the end of the meal, but if this keeps somebody running in and out of the kitchen or encourages those who probably are watching their weight to eat too much, it's misguided hospitality. What can be an inspiration to the cook is to see how even a modest wine can make a dish taste so much better – and, of course, many quite everyday recipes do involve the use of a little wine in the cooking.

You could, to ring the changes on the sessions, suggest that friends each bring a bottle they'd think suited to a particular dish: what wine would go best with, say, baked ham garnished with peaches? Or a range of Chinese dishes – either from your own wok or a nearby take away? Can you serve any wine with smoked mackerel, smoked trout or smoked eel – and if so, which wine? Is there an ideal wine for quiche Lorraine and, if so, will the same wine go equally well with asparagus or mushroom quiche? Solving the endless 'what with what' problems is a good notion for friends who often entertain each other.

GLASSES

There are specially shaped glasses made in some wine regions for the local wines. But there's no need to have more than one basic glass in use for wine – this can cost pence or pounds and you can buy it from a chain store or kitchen supply shop as well as from any specialist store.

The purpose of the glass is to make the wine more interesting and enjoyable. This means that the glass must help you to look at the wine's colour, sniff its smell, easily get it into your mouth. The ideal is either what is referred to as the 'tulip' shape, or else the rounder 'Paris goblet', which is rather like an onion with the top cut off. This type of glass is suitable for every kind of wine – still, sparkling, vermouth, fortified wines.

The glass should be of moderate size – neither too big nor too small. This is because, in order to get the smell of the wine, you are going to swing it round in the bowl of the glass, when the smell will be increased and released, channelled upwards to your nose. The glass should, therefore, never be more than half or two-thirds full, so that you can do this. Indeed, for a 'tasting sample' there will be much less in the glass. Don't suppose that by pouring only a moderate amount of wine you're going to look mean – the person who requires a glass filled to the brim obviously doesn't know anything about wine and won't be able to get any impression of the smell – or 'bouquet' as it is often termed.

So a glass that's too small not only means you'll pour a mean measure, but, if you try to swing the wine inside around, you may swirl it out of the glass altogether. The approximate size for every type of wine is $4 - 5\frac{1}{2}$ fluid ounces overall, which means when the glass is full to the brim. Less than that is too small, more is silly – the 'storm lantern' type of goldfish bowls used in some fancy restaurants that ought to know better. Not only are huge glasses clumsy to handle, but they can expose the wine to too much air which is just as bad as not letting it get any aeration at all.

Sometimes people hesitate about buying what seem biggish glasses, but in fact they're far more practical than the tiny or huge type. You can calculate quantities of wine per bottle if you have the 5 oz glass size (remember, you'll only pour about $2\frac{1}{2}$ oz of wine into the glass at one time) and, when you have a party, it's surprising how wine goes further when served in the sensibly sized glass: tiny glasses tend to get topped up constantly, sometimes more often than people really want, big glasses risk being knocked over. So invest in even the cheapest basic shape and size.

The all-purpose wine glass is on a stem. This means that, if you want a cool white or rosé wine, you don't have to put your hand round the bowl of the glass. But the stem also makes it easy to swirl the wine around and release the smell – you've paid for this, remember!

The all-purpose wine glass is of clear glass. You've paid for the colour of the wine and you ought to be able to see it. I know – some people do like the shimmer of cut glass, but this does slightly take away from the wine itself. (Use your cut-glass treasures for water or, of course, for a jug, carafe or decanter.) The Victorians, who put petticoats around table legs, used tinted wine glasses so that their eyes were not affronted by 'bits'. Today, modern filtration makes it unlikely that this is going to worry you – though remember that very fine wines may well have some deposit or the 'flyers' that occasionally appear. This doesn't mean that the wine is in any way 'off' (see pp. 43–46).

If possible, the glass should not only be clear but thin. This, though, is a counsel of perfection. But some cheap glasses do have a rather thickish rim, which you can't help being aware of when you're drinking. Sometimes they are also made of greyish-toned glass. Try to avoid this if you can. Fine crystal is a luxury to drink from – the very finest wine glasses are so thin that they give to the pressure of the hand! You are hardly aware of the contact of the glass with your mouth, only of the wine. But this is something very special – and although there are people who put their crystal glasses into the washing machine, for everyday purposes the cheaper type of glass is what everyone uses.

The bowl of the glass should curve slightly inwards – as it does in the tulip-shaped glass or Paris goblet. This is so that the smell of the wine is funnelled towards you, instead of escaping past your ears, and so that the wine itself is directed to your lips. There are some modern designs of wine glasses that have straight up and down sides and they can be used – although, for choice, you'll probably find that the curved bowl is the easiest shape from which to taste and to drink.

Glasses give light, elegance and sheen to a set table – it's always pleasant to see them and to use them. Try an experiment; put in a line a thick coloured tumbler (use plastic if you have one), a pottery cup and a wine glass. Pour a little wine into each – and sample it. The pleasure of the sight of the wine in the glass, the way in which you sniff the bouquet as you swirl it round and the ease and enjoyment with which the liquid then comes into your mouth – as if trying to please you – will be obvious.

Care of glasses

Even the cheapest glass, like the cheapest wine, benefits from being treated properly. A dusty, grease-smeared glass isn't attractive in itself and you certainly don't feel tempted to drink anything from it. A glass should be gleaming clean.

Whether you use soap, detergent or merely hot water, it's important always to rinse a glass thoroughly as anything remaining on it can smell and taint any subsequent wine. Even if grease clings to it or gets on from the drying cloth, it can 'flatten' the finest Champagne and sometimes even turn it a horrible drab pink. If possible, keep glass cloths only for drying and polishing glasses and, when you wash them, rinse them very thoroughly indeed and don't put them in a drawer or the linen cupboard where they come into contact with anything that smells – this can come off on the glass and no wine benefits by being lavender-scented! The best type of glass cloths are linen and these are often available with any 'dressing' already removed, so that they're ready for use. When you dry or polish a glass, don't put your thumb into it – sooner or later you'll pull the side of the glass out and you may cut yourself. Stuff the cloth into the bowl of the glass and turn it round to remove all the wet. If you can't wash up soon after a meal, fill the glasses with warm water to the brim and leave them standing up – when you later empty them, they won't bear streaks and marks as they will if you rinse them and leave them to drain without drying.

Storing glasses

Don't up-end glasses when you put them away. The air trapped inside them can cling when you use them again. If they rest on a pine shelf in a cupboard, then you may well wonder why an otherwise good wine reeks of something that reminds you of retsina! If you up-end glasses on plastic, it's even worse – you'll have to wash them again before you can use them. Test it: up-end a glass on an ordinary wooden shelf (it's likely to be pine), another glass on a plastic mat and a third on a piece of cloth or blotting-paper. After ten minutes, pick up the glasses and smell them . . . they'll stink! When you put them away, keep them upright and, if you're afraid of dust getting in, put a piece of ordinary copy paper lightly across the tops. Note the way glasses in many wine bars and pubs are kept in racks so that they hang upside down, but exposed to the air – they won't smell when you use them. But it's always wise to give any glass a preliminary sniff – glasses can pick up the smells of a carton, if they come to you for a party in a pack of the kind that is used for hiring them. If you can't wash them, then swing them about in the air. But for your own home use, keep them upright and away from wood, plastic or anything that may taint them.

Stains on glass

Sometimes decanters, jugs and carafes used for red wine, which have not been washed out at once after use, get stained. If ordinary washing won't shift the stain, try any preparation that's sold for cleaning false teeth – and rinse very well after the stain has vanished. Always try to clean a jug, decanter or carafe immediately after use – and make sure that it's dry inside; a dribble of stale water in a decanter can make a fine wine taste horrible. Up-end the decanter on a clean glass cloth until it's completely dry.

Lipstick

Some guests may leave very definite traces of lipstick on wine glasses. It really isn't necessary to do this – most good lipsticks, when properly applied and blotted, will do no more than possibly make a slightly greasy mark on the side of the glass. In the ordinary way, if each person has his or her own glass, this shouldn't present problems – but perhaps it's worth mentioning that there are plenty of women who, at professional tastings, use the same glass as other tasters and don't leave any traces at all. It *can* be done!

OPENING THE BOTTLE

Like many routine procedures, there's a right and a wrong way – and the right way is the easiest. For preparing the wine beforehand as regards temperature see page 46.

First, get yourself an efficient corkscrew. Many are definitely bad – if the screw has a pointed end, it will merely bore a hole through the cork and if the screw is sharp edged, this will cut into the cork and, sometimes, make it crumble, at other times just break up the cork as it is pushed in. The ideal corkscrew has a rounded screw that will grip and hold the cork; the end curls round so that you can look up the spiral – like looking up a spiral staircase. There are many variations on the basic corkscrew, some with levers that heave the cork out, one device that has a 'reverse screw' that you turn once the screw is firmly in the cork, another that you go on screwing in and that raises the cork effortlessly. Get a correctly shaped corkscrew – it will save you effort and broken corks. Always wipe the top of the capsule first. Either remove the entire capsule or cut off the top, which is why many 'waiter's friend' corkscrews have a penknife included. The capsule should be cut below the lip of the bottle, so that when the wine is poured it won't flow over the capsule – metal and plastic can affect the taste. Plastic capsules are often perforated with the aim of making them easier to remove – but they are usually tough on the finger-nails anyway. Wipe the top of the cork.

Insert the corkscrew in the centre of the cork and turn it steadily until it gets just to the bottom of the cork – ideally, not piercing the base. But it doesn't matter if this does occur, although you may get a bit of cork falling into the wine. (This won't make the wine 'corked' at all – see pp. 45.) Then pull the cork. If it is hard to extract, put the bottle on the floor and, with one hand pulling, push down on the bottle with the other hand, to get double force. Wipe the inside of the neck of the bottle. There are three 'wipes' you should always make when opening a bottle: sometimes there may be dust on the capsule, sometimes 'gunge', slightly wet, on the top of the cork, some-times a little deposit in the bottle neck. Wipe them away.

If you find a cork is very hard to budge (as can happen with a young wine) remove the corkscrew and re-insert it diagonally across the cork, to get extra leverage.

If the cork breaks or crumbles, wipe off the bits, then put the corkscrew back and gently remove the rest of the cork. If you can't manage this, push it down into the wine and, when you're making the first pouring, do so gently, so that the cork, bobbing in the wine, doesn't block up the neck of the bottle. After a bit, it will flow normally – and the cork in the wine doesn't make the wine 'corked'. If a lot of tiny bits get into the wine, then it is a good idea to filter the wine into a jug, carafe, clean bottle or decanter. There are various ways of doing this, but the simplest for most people is to use a fine plastic filter, the type available from any kitchen supplier, which you should not use for anything else except wine and which must be cleaned with hot water every time you use it and put away so that it doesn't take on any other smells in the kitchen. This filter can also be used if you're tipping out the dregs of a bottle, where there may be some deposit, and using the wine up in cooking or to make vinegar. Never use any type of opener that involves pumping gas into a wine if you are opening a bottle of even slightly sparkling wine – such as Mateus Rosé or a vinho verde and certainly *never* for a sparkling wine. Such an opener, which can be used for still wines, can make a bottle of sparkling wine explode and can do serious damage.

Opening sparkling wines

Never open any bottle of sparkling wine without holding the bottle in a cloth. Bottles seldom split these days – but it can happen and the risk to your hand is serious.

Tilt the bottle away from you and so that it doesn't point at anyone or anything. (Every year, people lose eyes by being careless in this way.) Untwist the wire 'muzzle', usually anti-clockwise, but not always. From the instant this wire is loosened, *do not let go of the top of the cork* – you have in your hand something that can fly out like a bullet. Hold on to the top of the 'mushroom' of the cork and, with your other hand, gently turn the bottle. *Turn the bottle, not the cork.* If you try to turn the cork, you'll probably break off the top of the 'mushroom'. The cork should gradually be eased up from the bottle and emerge with a discreet 'burp' – it's not only silly and risky to 'pop' a cork, a lot of wine may rush out and be wasted. Have a glass nearby and pour the wine into it, then into other glasses. The wine may foam up and out of the bottle, so pour at once.

If the cork sticks hard, you will be able to loosen it by letting a stream of hot water run onto the neck of the bottle for a few seconds. But *don't let go of the cork*. The heat, increasing the pressure behind the cork, will push it out.

If you do break off the top of the mushroom, then you must

pierce the rest of the cork, wait until you hear the 'hiss' as the pressure behind it is released, and then use a corkscrew in the ordinary way. *Remember* that if you've carried a bottle of sparkling wine home in your basket or the boot of your car, the wine will be extra 'lively' and the cork may fly out even more suddenly than usual – shaking the wine up increases the pressure. Be even more careful *not to let go of the cork*.

WHEN THERE'S

SOMETHING WRONG

Although faulty bottles are inclined to be rare these days, you can find the odd one, and it usually happens on the very occasion when you're either giving an important meal or else in the sort of restaurant where you're the host and responsible for guests getting the best you can afford.

When do you send the bottle back, to the shop or the restaurant 'despense'? First of all, make sure that it is the bottle you originally ordered. This can happen in a busy eating-place, when a bottle gets into the wrong bin, which is why the wine waiter should always show ('present') the bottle to you before your nod of approval permits him to draw the cork. Check that it's the wine you want, the vintage (if any) you chose from the list, the source of supply (shipper, merchant or grower) as named on the list. If it isn't, ask why. No-one is likely to say, 'It's a rather second-rate version of the wine on the list, but perfectly adequate,' although it might be more sensible if they did. But unless they can provide a reasonable explanation: the vintage has changed (but is it one you still think you'd like?), the grower or original supplier has been changed but perhaps for the better (well, give them the benefit of the doubt if the price is the same), the original wine was so popular it simply ran out and this is what the establishment hopes will be as pleasant (again, it's up to you to try it without prejudice), or – and sometimes you'll have to do this – order another wine that *is* the same as the wine on the list. Of course, if you know and trust the wine merchant or the wine waiter, you can probably go along with him encouraging you to try something slightly different. Then, does the wine look, smell and taste healthy? If it's all cloudy and of a curious colour, you may be right to object. A little experience can easily familiarise you with what most wines should be like – just because the smell seems unusual, or there is a lot of deposit in your glass (the fault of the waiter who didn't handle it carefully), or the taste isn't wholly and immediately agreeable, don't always assume that this is the fault of the wine. It may be simply that you don't like it! Or you've been eating or drinking things that have made it difficult for you to appreciate a particular wine; two or three strong cocktails can 'smash' the delicate light wines, so that they disappoint you. If you've been drinking a slightly sweet apéritif (such as a 'medium' sherry, or one of the slightly sweet wine-based proprietory drinks), don't blame a truly dry wine for seeming 'acid and bitter' if you try it immediately after this. Also, do check whether or not, in a restaurant, you may have a glass that has tainted the wine; this can easily happen. The thing to do is to try to rinse the glass thoroughly with the wine – move the wine around in the glass, so that it moistens the whole bowl, right up to the rim. All right – in a restaurant it can delay things and it takes some nerve – but who's paying the bill?

Things that signal trouble

If you're sure that the wine is what you ordered or bought, that there's nothing the matter with the glass and that you're in a reasonable state of mind and palate to enjoy the contents of the bottle, then you can be fair about your preliminary tasting.

Is the wine, if white, dark in tone and brownish? This can mean that it is either very old stock or has somehow been exposed to light and, even, air. Distinguish between a beautiful golden and a dull, faded colour of any white wine. Even the cheapest wine should look bright and, somehow, 'living', not flat – think of the stale water in a carafe as compared with spring water. Does it smell healthy? Well, what's 'healthy'? A wine should have a fresh, clean, moderately agreeable smell – any real stink means that it should be rejected. But suppose it doesn't smell at all? That can be because it needs a bit of aeration, but if, after you swing it round in the glass, it still doesn't 'give' of any smell, that is something of a warning. Leave it for a few moments, then sniff it again. You may find that a completely different smell emerges from the glass.

Remember, the 'bottle stink' of the stale air kept in the bottle under the cork can, when the cork is first drawn, smell like – well, like stale air – and this will pass in a few minutes. But what I can only describe as a negative absence of smell is rather different. All wine should have a smell. Good wine has a bouquet, possibly also an aroma, some have a perfume – goodness, how complicated it sounds. Use your nose when trying a bottle – if the smell suggests anything unclean, soggy, dirty, disagreeable to you (although don't be put off by smells that are merely unusual), then put the glass down and, later, try it once more. You may then decide to reject the wine – or discover that, although strange, it's most interesting to drink as well as to smell.

The flavour should also be clean and agreeable. You know what good food is like, as compared with second-rate, pretentious food? Wine's the same.

A wine that is 'corked' won't necessarily smell of cork. Sometimes it does. Sometimes, at least to me, it acquires a sharp, chemical smell that evokes the chlorine of a swimming-bath. It won't harm you if you drink it, but it isn't pleasant. In general, if a wine developes this acrid, harsh smell and flat, vaguely chemical flavour, it's not as it should be. What do you do? Easy to say but not always easy to do. (Try being the guest who *knows* a bottle is 'off' when a host has approved it and you love them dearly!) If you are in a restaurant, tell the wine waiter that the bottle is not as it should be and it will then be taken away and another (or a different wine, if you order one) will replace it. The defective bottle will be returned to the source of supply and will not be charged to you. With shop-bought wine, take the bottle back, and say why. Ideally, do this as soon as possible. *Don't* drink all of it except the last inch and then return it with the comment, 'I think that this was not quite right' – if it wasn't right, why did you drink it?

Never blame the supplier – wine is an odd thing and, whereas the most aristocratic cellars can, occasionally, issue bottles that prove to be less perfect than they should be, so the most impeccable installations likewise may (no one ever can find out why) put out wines that show some defect. But as you can always have your bottle replaced, free of charge, this need not be a problem. (Although it does reinforce my theory that one should never buy a single bottle at a time if this is going to be served at a meal to which you invite guests – how terrible if the one bottle is 'off' and there isn't another!)

HANDLING AND SERVING

You've paid for the wine, now you have a part to play so as to get the wine to provide you with maximum enjoyment; this means paying some attention to how you serve it. There's nothing complicated about any of the routine procedures, indeed, it's usually the wine snobs and the wine bores, rather than those who really do know something about wine, who make a fuss about presentation.

If possible, stand the bottle of wine upright for some hours before you plan to draw the cork. With a red wine, put the bottle in the room in which you are going to drink it.

Temperature

White, sparkling, and pink wines and vermouth: White and sparkling and pink wines and vermouth are all most enjoyable if they are cool, but this means lightly chilled, not frozen stiff. Indeed, if a wine is virtually iced, it's impossible to enjoy the smell. What you aim for is that the wine should be agreeably fresh and cold as it enters your mouth – not so cold that it makes your teeth ache! All wines served as apéritifs should be cool, to perk up the taste buds. Temperature is relative – to you and the heat of your room and to the weather. On a stuffy day, it may be more agreeable to have your apéritifs and any other white or sparkling wines slightly cooler than on a crisp cold winter day. A truly sweet luscious wine is also probably most enjoyable if served colder than a light, delicate dry wine. Experiment – see how the wine shows itself off when cool as compared with tepid leftover wine. Don't put ice in the wine as this merely dilutes the drink.

In theory, 10 – 14°C is usually the pleasantest temperature for dry, sparkling and rosé wines, unless the weather is really hot or, as can happen even in winter, it's a stuffy day. Very sweet wines can be a little colder. But the best way of judging is to put your hand on the bottle and see if it feels agreeably cold, although not iced. If you use a refrigerator, put the bottle in for about an hour – a little longer on a very hot or stuffy day, or if you are chilling a sweet wine. If you have an ice bucket, put a mixture of ice and water in this, not ice alone, which will merely chill patches of the bottle. Then plunge the bottle in so that the level of the ice and water comes up to the level of the wine in the bottle. If an ordinary ice bucket isn't deep enough, use any bucket or, at worst, put the bottle in upside down; I know – when you pour the wine, the liquid will turn round in the bottle, but at least it will run through the already chilled neck of the bottle. If only the bottom part of the bottle is chilled, then the first glass or more will not be chilled at all.

In an ice bucket, the temperature of the wine in the bottle will be brought down much faster than in a refrigerator – about 12 – 15 minutes will be enough for all but a very sweet wine. Draw the cork a few minutes ahead of time – this will get rid of any stale air imprisoned in the bottle. Don't ever put a bottle of wine in the freezer – frozen wine never tastes quite right even when it thaws. But, on a hot day and if you're in a hurry, it can help to put the wine glasses in the fridge. They go pearly when the wine is poured and add to the cooling. Don't forget that a bottle left in the ice bucket will go on getting cooler – so on a cold day you may take it out once you've achieved a satisfactory cool temperature.

Red wines: The ideal way to serve most red wines, as you probably know, is at 'room temperature' or 'chambré'. But some peoples' rooms are kept at a higher temperature than others. The fact is that most red wines, although not all, are more enjoyable if they have had a little exposure to air, so as to 'breathe', when they will give off their pleasant smell and the taste will be more obvious. With some of the most famous fine wines – outside the scope of our tastings here – several hours aeration may be required to bring them happily to peak enjoyment, but in general the important thing to bear in mind is that a red wine should be agreeable to smell and to taste. This enjoyment is achieved quite simply, but never make the mistake of deliberately heating up a wine, even if you've just brought it from a cold cellar; if you stand it in front of the fire it'll merely get scorched on one side of the bottle, if you put it up above the kitchen stove, then it will only get a vaguely warm character – and do you want it to taste like mulled wine? The risk of doing this is that, once a wine is heated, you can't restore it to its former pleasantness.

If you've got time, stand the bottle in the room where you're going to drink the wine and draw the cork (see pp. 40) an hour or two in advance of when you want to taste or drink. The wine will take on the temperature of the room and the removal of the cork will all get rid of any stale air under the cork in the bottle – which is known as 'bottle stink'. (Ideally, you should also draw the cork of a white wine in advance too.) With some rather 'important' and special wines, you may wish to decant them. This is quite easy and the additional aeration can be beneficial. Some people suppose that only wines with a deposit need decanting, but pouring a wine through air gets it 'chambré' in an ideal and rapid way, and you may like to show off the beautiful colour in an elegant decanter. If you haven't got a decanter, use a carafe or glass jug or simply a clean, rinsed bottle.

Decanting

Draw the cork in the usual way (see pp. 40). Have the decanter or carafe plus a wine glass and a source of light all at hand on a table where you are going to decant. The light can be a candle, but also a torch laid on its side, a bicycle lamp or, if you wish, a table lamp with the shade removed. The thing to aim at is to have a source of light that will show you the clarity or other-wise of the wine as it flows from bottle to decanter. Lift the bottle carefully and hold it so that the light shines through the neck of the bottle. Then begin to pour, steadily and without splashing or slopping the wine back up and down in the bottle – this will only churn up any slight deposit that may be there and the whole wine will be cloudy.

Don't stop for anything less than a life or death emergency once you start to pour! (And, if you're using a candle, be careful not to drip any wine onto it and put it out.)

Once you see any trace of dusty deposit or sludge coming up into the neck of the bottle, keep the bottle still, but inclined, and move it from the decanter or carafe and pour the remain-der of the wine into the wine glass. If the wine becomes very 'thick', stop pouring and put the bottle down. But you can often get a lot more wine out of a bottle if you pour carefully at the end and the wine in the glass can then be used to try the taste and, if you wish, added to the wine in the decanter. There is sometimes just a drop or two that is cloudy or with deposit in it even in a cheap wine, so it's worth keeping the wine 'bright' and using the wine with deposit for cooking. This is why, when you pour a red wine, it's usually wise never to pour every drop out into the glasses unless you are quite sure it's what is known as 'star bright' to the last.

Red wines that are pleasant served cool

Some red wines, especially those that are most delightful because of their fruity flavour, are often served as they might come from a cool cellar – this brings out the crisp, lip-smacking character. (Try eating chilled fruit and see how much nicer it usually tastes.) This sort of wine can be lightly chilled, especially in hot weather. Such wines include young Beaujolais, many of the young red wines of the Loire, such as Chinon, or Loire Gamay wines and, with all inexpensive reds, there's no reason why they shouldn't be served at cellar temperature if you think they're nicer that way. After all, people can always put their hands round the bowl of the glass to warm them up if they wish – but no one who knows anything about wine ever asks for a wine to be 'warmed'; they will either wait for it to get to room temperature, or put their hands round the glass. That's the way to 'chambré' a wine, rather than bringing it abruptly to almost blood heat – you do need to know when it enters your mouth, after all!

BUYING THE WINE FOR THE TASTING
SESSIONS

All the wines you're going to try are 'table wines' – made to be drunk with food or, if you wish, by themselves. They come into the 'light wine' category according to strength – not exceeding 14.5° in terms of percentage of alcohol by volume – and pay 'light wine' duty. We shall not deal with the 'heavy wines', such as port, sherry and Madeira. This is not to say they are not worth attention; but space restricts the scope of this book.

Vermouth will, however, be included (you'll see why when you get to it) and some sparkling wines.

Nearly all the wines will be widely available and, for each tasting session, those to be tasted and drunk will all come from the same retail outlet. In case you can't get to this particular shop, there are a few alternative suggestions, though do bear in mind that, even with wines bearing the same names, there will be differences according to who does the buying for that retailer. For example, Sainsbury's Muscadet will not be exactly the same Muscadet as that of Peter Dominic, nor will one shop's 'house red' be the same as the 'house red' of the shop in the next street belonging to a different owner. The branded wines, such as Sichel's Blue Nun Liebfraumilch, of course, will be the same wherever you find them – but another firm's Liebfraumilch may be very different, even though it quite legally carries the same wine name on the label. This is rather like people in a family – there may be a distinct family resemblance, but there may not.

Vintage and non-vintage

There's an odd snobbery about 'vintage wines'. But the majority of the wines of the world are non-vintage, ready for immediate enjoyment when offered for sale. There are two points about wines that have a vintage date: the first is for the very fine wines that may improve if able to be stored to gain additional 'bottle age'. The vintage date will indicate how old the wine is, also give some idea as to the sort of vintage when it was made – very long-lived, likely to be at its best short-term, easy-going and sunny or perhaps rather hard and firm. Wines don't go on getting better – indeed, they can decline after reaching their peak, so age is not invariably a good thing; some wines, from some vintages, may be at their best within a few years, others may require keeping for some time to show off their very best.

The other usefulness of the vintage date is to show how old a wine is – when it happens to be one of those wines that will be most enjoyable when drunk while still young. With certain white wines, for example, such as an inexpensive Sauvignon (see p. 105) the wine will darken in colour and lose its fresh, zippy charm and delightful fruity taste if kept too long. The vintage date is a guide to prevent you buying something that's 'over the top'. So don't be too insistent that 'It must be a vintage wine'. Indeed, if you get certain vintage dates put on certain bottles, they may indicate a rather poor vintage when, although some adequate wine has been made, in general the wines will not be more than drinkable, nothing special.

Most Champagne and sparkling wines are non-vintage, so are the 'everyday' table wines that are blended, year by year, so as to ensure continuity of style; once a wine has established itself as a popular drink, consumers don't want suddenly to find it completely different in character. Sometimes the producers of the 'big blends' do alter the style of their wines a bit, either buying from a different source of supply, or improving the wine by various methods; customers may notice a slight difference, but nothing marked. What you may notice, however, is that very occasionally you do get a bottle that you usually enjoy that is 'not as usual' and this may be either because it's been kept too long in stock and lost its freshness, been inadvertently subjected to poor conditions (being under a strong light, standing up, for some while). Even in the best-run retailers, this can sometimes happen, but unless the wine is really 'off' (see pp. 43–46), when you should return it, the difference may not make it wholly unacceptable.

How many bottles and how much

There are about six to eight helpings, for people drinking, out of most wine bottles. For sample tasting portions, you should get 16 – 18. This is when you pour the wine into the adequately sized glass. You can work out how much wine you'll need in advance and remember that any not used can remain in the recorked bottle, kept in a cool place, to be used 24 hours later, as you wish. It will remain perfectly drinkable; sometimes it may even seem more enjoyable after 'breathing' for some while. If possible, though, don't leave a previously opened bottle like this when you've already drunk more than half the contents – the amount of air in the bottle will affect it, so it's ideal, if you have an empty half bottle, to put the remaining wine into this until you wish to finish it.

With drinks before a meal, which is probably when you'll be doing your tasting, it's usually sound to allow the equivalent of

$1\frac{1}{2}$ – 2 normal helpings of wine before you start the food. Of course, if you only have two wines to taste, this is easy to calculate as regards the tasting samples; with more wines, work out the small helpings (ideally, have one person pouring to supervise the 'portion control') so that people can try all the wines. If, however, you're including a sweet wine in the set of tasting samples, have a little pause and recommend people to have something to nibble before they go to the food and the first wine again – otherwise, if you start with a dry wine, it may taste bitter and sharp after anything slightly sweet. Generally, people will drink 3 – 4 glasses of wine with a meal, although on special occasions it's probably prudent to allow 6 – 8. After all, you'll probably take a couple of hours or more over this kind of meal. When there are two or more wines with food, the tendency is to drink more of the second wine or the last wine. If, however, for our special occasions, you see that there is one definitely special wine, then 'introduce it' with something that can be drunk in fairly generous quantities, so that the top wine, which will probably be the most expensive one, can be saved.

Buying

In many retail wine shops you'll get a 'case discount' if you buy a case of a dozen bottles of wine at a time. Some firms will grant this on a mixed case, others not. Ask, or read the conditions of sale in their wine list. For a large-scale party, wine can usually be supplied on a 'sale or return' basis, which means that you can take back afterwards any unopened bottles (with undamaged labels) that you haven't used. A super-market, however, may not be able to give a case discount, because, reasonably enough, they have already pared down their margins of profit as far as is possible. In many instances, firms can arrange to deliver wine to your home, sometimes without charge if you are near enough to them. Posting wines, however, is costly. Supermarkets often have arrangements whereby customers can collect heavy loads – such as wine – at special loading bays, with staff to help you heave the wine into your car or taxi or shopping trolley.

What and when

In the following tasting sessions, there's no need to go straight through, section by section. If you wish, look up one session that concentrates on what you think may be specially interesting or topical for you or, otherwise, try one of the more routine sessions or, if you've gone through this already, vary it by selecting some of the alternative choices among the bottles. It's also rewarding and, often, revealing to try exactly the same wines after an interval – they may seem different at different times of the year or you may approach them with a different attitude and the gained experience that may enlighten – as well as enliven – your opinions about them.

NOTES, TERMS AND WINE WORDS

If you can, do make a note of what you're tasting while or immediately after you are trying it. Even half an hour later your impressions will not be as clear. Some indication of your reactions, for good or bad, can be of great use when you're next buying wine, so can any extra information, such as 'Excellent with baked fish', 'A bit light for veal and ham pie, but would go well with quiche Lorraine or a light pâté', 'The combination of this wine with that casserole was first-rate.'

It isn't really helpful simply to note 'Nice', or 'Didn't like'. Try to attach some sort of tag to each wine if you can. Don't bother to write copious tasting notes if you don't feel inclined, but if a wine's colour is especially attractive, or its bouquet reminds you of a particular fragrance – say, of a flower – and if the flavour seems unexpectedly fruity, or full, or much sweeter or drier than you'd first anticipated, jot down your reactions. Don't spend too much time about this. Remember, your tasting notes are for your eyes only. If you are comparing your experiences with friends, it's fine to quote from them, but *they* can't taste for you, even if they may have hit on a really evocative description. Use your own language.

There is today a tendency among enthusiastic tasters to refine a great deal on basic smells and flavours. Some books go into great detail about this, differentiating between, for example, different sorts of fruit, the fur of various animals, various kinds of foliage, spices and the aromas and flavours of other beverages, such as coffee. Some authorities give long lists of the various smells and tastes, categorising them in relation to wines. Other people evolve complex terminology for themselves, and then expect the ordinary person to follow their meaning when they use these terms.

Now, everybody develops their own tasting vocabulary, even after quite a short period of enjoying wine. But it's personal for each drinker – unless, of course, you are involved in the wine trade or teaching students to get through examinations, when naturally there tends to be some common 'in language' that both candidates and examiners are able to use. For us ordinary people it's enough if we can make ourselves understood to each other – and to anyone from whom we are buying our wine. If someone says that a wine smells 'of apples', *they* may mean this is a pleasant smell; if I pick up what is an 'appley' smell in a wine, however, it suggests to me that there's something amiss, because there is a stage in the fermentation process when some wines smell rather like this, and they ought not to do so when they are in bottle, ready to drink. If I am trying to describe a wine that somebody else finds 'appley', I may use the terms 'crisp, zippy, clean, fresh' even 'green' which is a term often used by those who attempt to describe the different odours or perfumes – from wide usage, people usually accept its general significance; if they say a scent is 'warm', this suggests it is quite different from one that is 'green'. You see how difficult it is to explain or describe one set of sensations by means of mere words!

I do not like encouraging people to try to discover certain smell or taste associations merely by what I tell them; if they invent some word or phrase for themselves, it will mean much more. But straining to discover what is meant by a widely-used term when it doesn't mean much *to you* is not going to help you when you're not in contact with the appropriate reference book or a friendly instructor guiding you. My own teacher used to say firmly, 'If you're told you ought to find the Taj Mahal by moonlight in a particular wine – you'll find it! What good will that do you?' So, one taster's 'appley' may be another taster's 'crisp and crunchy' or another's 'fresh and slightly sharp' – or they may associate the wine with a fruit or flower.

All you're trying to do is to discover wines you like and

wines you don't like – and *why* you like or don't like them. As I've mentioned, you needn't go through the tasting sessions in order, but each one has a point to make about the wines: it may be the general style of a particular country or region, it may be an example of a classic wine grape that you can find in vineyards of many countries, it may be to demonstrate the enjoyable character of wines from fairly 'new' wine areas that you may have not previously tried. You can vary the food, you can vary the wines, subject to the notes that suggest alternatives.

In most wine books you get some kind of vocabulary or glossary. This will explain some technical terms and introduce the words often heard in the context of wine. In this book, you'll find all the special words you need in the various sessions, either explained within the text or defined separately. This enables you to concentrate on just a few pages at a time and doesn't burden you with lots of new words and phrases.

WHAT YOU NEED TO KNOW BEFORE
YOU BEGIN TASTING

What's in wine?

A bottle of wine can cost a couple of pounds, or a couple of hundred pounds, but between 85% and 90% of the wine itself is water. It's the remaining 'things' that make the differences between wines. These elements can vary enormously, but there are three main ones (unless you're a chemist and go into all the formulae and sub-divisions). These three are alcohol, acidity and sugar and in every single wine they should be there, in adequate proportions, so that the result is a 'balanced wine'. Don't try to taste deliberately looking out for them, as this will distract you, but if you particularly dislike a wine, then it's worth trying to see whether, for example, the acidity is too low, or there is too much sugar or what. So here are the elements and the parts they, discreetly, play. You'll see that there are plenty of examples, many in the average kitchen, that will help you register them in basic ways, so you won't have to waste any wine while you experiment.

Alcohol: This is what holds the wine together, just as the human skeleton holds the human body. It acts as a protection against various forms of infection and certain hazards, such as when a wine travels from one place to another. You can't tell the exact amount of alcohol in a wine merely by tasting it, unless there's so much that, as you drink, you have the sensation of flames coming out of your ears and no decent wine is made like that! There are different forms of alcohol and, if you use any spirit lamp, you'll certainly have registered the smell of methylated spirit (methyl alcohol). However, ethyl alcohol is the most prominent in wine. To register this, see what you think when you smell vodka; it will probably make your nose tingle slightly and it has an assertive, light, very 'clean' smell that goes on burrowing around your nose and the spaces inside your face where smells waft about. If you taste it, there may be an initial impression of sweetness on the tip of your tongue – where the tastebuds register sweetness – and then a feeling of slight oiliness. Don't worry if you can't register much from vodka but, if possible, see whether you get any impression from other spirits – borrow someone's glass to have a sniff – and see how the alcohol is, always, at the back of the other flavourings that you'll smell in gin, whisky, brandy. It's the alcohol that penetrates all the faculties you use in the sense of taste – see how it goes right to the back of your nose and throat, even if you've got the remains of other smells and flavours in your nose and mouth and have a slight cold or even a touch of catarrh! The 'fumes' of the alcohol are present, even though they can be underneath other, possibly more agreeable and complicated smells and tastes and, if you sniff at a completely empty glass in which a spirit has been, you will note how the fumes cling to the glass for a while.

Table wines are all within a quite short range of alcoholic strength and H. M. Customs & Excise levy higher duty on wines over the top limit. The indication you occasionally get that a wine is too high in alcohol to be balanced – in relation to the other elements – is if you seem to get a whiff of what you may now register as 'something strong' when you smell it and, when you drink it, you experience a slight 'hot' sensation. This is the alcohol pushing itself forward and, often, overpowering the other elements. This is unlikely in most wine of medium quality, though you may be aware of it if you buy anything very cheap from a hot vineyard region.

Acidity: Don't associate the term 'acid' or 'acidity' with anything disagreeable as it makes a most important contribution to wine of all types, from the very dry to the sweetest. Indeed, if alcohol is the bone structure of a wine, acidity is the nervous system; it gives a wine personality, intensity, definition, character, interest. The most obvious everyday example of acidity is a lemon – probably your mouth waters slightly even at the mention of this beautiful and endlessly useful fruit. Even a few drops of lemon juice can 'lift' a sauce, endow an ordinary recipe with subtle differences of taste, provide complexity to a routine dish, even if you can't definitely taste the lemon. Nearly all fruit demonstrates how acidity is so important. In the crisp, clean flavour of an apple or even in the sweetest and most luscious peach, there's something – the acidity – that prevents the ripe fruit from cloying and dulling the palate. You can register acidity in a good eating apple, such as a Cox, or, if you bite into a prime cooking apple, such as a Bramley, you can see how the tart, zippy flesh of the fruit has a definite flavour – it's not just woolly apple, such as you may get in a rather stale fruit of not such a good variety.

Wines that show marked acidity in various forms include most of those made from the Sauvignon grape; if you get an example of this from a fairly warm area, such as Bordeaux, which has a temperate climate, it may seem a little softer and less crisp, whereas a good Loire Sauvignon, such as one from Sancerre, will show off that extreme freshness that I often note as the 'green gooseberry' style. A Portuguese white vinho verde will also exemplify a pleasant acidity – look for this behind the mini-sparkle of the wine. But even quite a sweet wine will have adequate acidity; try one of the modestly-priced Sauternes and note how, at the back of the delectable lusciousness, there's a little firm, almost crisp 'something' that prevents the wine from seeming syrupy – that's the acidity. Red wines must also have sufficient acidity and you will note this in all of quality. The red Loire wines possibly demonstrate acidity to a marked extent, but you can also taste how there is adequate acidity folded in, as it were, to the flavours of claret, especially in a young wine, or note its presence in wines simply labelled 'Cabernet' from central Europe; this refers to the grape name, which, in this instance, will usually be the Caber-net Franc.

Don't be confused into supposing that acidity in a wine is the same thing as a wine that is 'acetic'. This last means that the wine is on the way to becoming vinegar. Most people know the sharp smell of wine vinegar, but no wine should have this smell. Wine can become vinegar as the result of bacterial action and this is why, in places where wine is made, no old or stale wine that might be 'turning', or any vinegar itself should be in even remote contact with the new wine, for fear of infecting it. Sometimes you may find that a wine gives you a faint whiff that evokes the smell of vinegar – this may indicate that it is getting dangerously near turning into vinegar itself.

Sugar: There's some sugar even in the very driest wine. Indeed, it's as important as acidity and alcohol. The two main sugars are glucose and fructose, and, as sugar is an essential in fruit, even in the tartest, crispest fruit you can find, they are present in wine. It's the sugar in proportion to the acidity that gives the balance to a wine, if one examines the taste in detail – note how the fruitiness and acidity are so agreeably combined in an enjoyable wine, dry or sweet. If you are able to think of the alcohol as the skeleton of the wine, the acidity as the nervous system, then the fruit (of which sugar is an example) is the flesh. This is why very old wines, past their best, 'dry out'. Just as the skin and flesh of a human being wrinkles, dries out and shrivels as that person gets old, so the sugar/fruit declines and the wine can get hard, dry and sharp (out of balance). Sometimes you can even get a trace of the alcohol coming through, as the bone structure does when somebody is very old and debilitated.

Most people will be quite clear in their minds what sugar is. Grapes are high in sugar, although wine grapes are seldom sweet enough to play a double part and be enjoyed as table grapes. The natural sugar in grapes provides the quick restorative 'lift' to a human being, which is why traditionally grapes are given to invalids or convalescents; before sugar was cheap, they were a natural source of glucose and fructose.

You can't in fact smell pure glucose, but there are plenty of wines that are lip-smackingly fruity. Only the boys in white coats in the laboratories can analyse the exact sugar in wine, but there are many obvious examples, even from wines that many people would consider 'dry'. Beaujolais and any wines made from the Gamay grape are enjoyably fruity, so are wines made from the Riesling grape, Muscat – to drink a wine made from the Muscat is like crunching into a bunch of grapes – and, of course, wines that come into the category of 'late picked', when the slightly overripe grapes give them a delicious sweetness.

When you hear wine talk, there are a few other terms that may crop up and are not difficult to understand.

Tannin: This is the astringent element, that 'pulls' the mouth slightly, as when you drink very strong tea or eat rhubarb. It is particularly present in many wines that are capable of improving with time; many people who taste very fine wines while these are young don't like them and often term them 'harsh'; this is because of the tannin. Tannin will keep a wine and, as the wine ages, the tannic attribute will soften and almost disappear as the wine comes to its prime. You can register tannin particularly with wines made from or with a high proportion of Cabernet Sauvignon grapes, such as young claret (red Bordeaux). They can, when immature, be rather like gawky young people – all bones and awkwardness, but, to the discerning, promise great future potential. Don't confuse tannin with acidity – acidity is crisp and cleanly sharp, tannin is often registered with the lips and the sides of the mouth, puckering the tender skin.

Aldehydes and esters: These contribute to the character of the bouquet of a wine – if you enjoy the wine's smell, you are probably enjoying them. But unless you are chemically inclined, this is all that you need to know about them.

Glycerine: This is something that is formed from sugar during the process of fermentation. Many people suppose that it is glycerine that causes the trails of transparent viscosity that one can often note on the sides of a wine glass, after you have swirled the wine around. In fact these trails (see p. 177) are a manifestation of ethyl alcohol. But glycerine does contribute to the smoothness and fatness of many wines.

NOTES ON

THE TASTING SESSIONS

The following sessions have been planned so that you can learn about the more important wine grapes, styles of wines and how these can be affected by vineyard conditions and make the acquaintance of wines from all over the world to vary your selection. Each session features wines from one retail outlet – except for the opening session, which is about two widely-stocked wines – but of course every single shop may not always have all the wines in stock; they may, however, be able to order from headquarters on request. Suggestions for alternative wines are made, but of course the tasting notes cannot usually be exactly applied to all of these. Some wines that are not featured, although mentioned, include US wines, because these tend to be so affected by the rate of the US dollar against the pound sterling that they may be disproportionately expensive when you buy them here. English wines are not included, because, obviously, supplies vary considerably, but they are quite widely available these days. Wines that vary very much in style from vintage to vintage have also been omitted, because the difference between one vintage and another can be very great. But you should be able to get a general impression, on a small scale, of such wines from sessions featuring either the non-vintage versions or wines made from classic grapes coming from vineyards where there is not too much difference between one year and another. It's always possible to check with a merchant or the vintage reports now available in specialised magazines or wine lists as to the sort of wine that is likely to suit your requirements in this category. Very expensive and rare wines have not been discussed here, although many of the retailers mentioned will have at least some; but supplies of these can change – there are not limitless amounts of fine wines – and so it's up to you to look out for this sort of bottle and, if possible, ask advice before you buy.

All the retail outlets will also have a range of everyday wines which they sell either under brands, or simply as 'House red', 'House white'. These have not been included, because I've assumed that, if you buy from a particular shop anyway, you'll probably already have purchased some of their popular and cheap wines – it's by wines at the bottom of the price ranges that the skill and dedication of the buyer is to be judged. Also, whereas the 'House rosé' of one firm may, at one time, come from one region, or one country, changes of various kinds may cause the source of supply to be changed and naturally the wine's basic character may be different. This is another reason for never deciding once and for all that you don't like a particular brand of wine or a firm's speciality! Try it again from time to time.

Generally, the medium priced wines do have more to offer the drinker in terms both of interest and additional sensations of taste than the very cheapest wines, which is why these are the wines on which these sessions concentrate. You do, as a wine lover, want to talk about what you drink as well as just enjoying it; this is why some background information is provided. Of course, much more could be said, but if you're seriously interested, it's to be hoped that you'll go on to read about these wines for yourself.

Limitations of space have also prevented the inclusion of more of the good retail chains in which Britain is so fortunate, but this should not prevent the readers of this book from experimenting with the wines of as many merchants as possible. There will not be many these days who are restricted to a single source of supply, although of course some have more retailers to draw on than others.

The foods suggested attempt to cope with the problems of those who want to eat very well, those who are limited as to time and money, and those who require the food after a tasting to be really simple and trouble-free; this is why take-aways, delicatessen foods and very basic family fare feature here as well as elaborate menus. Informal occasions are included, also several buffet meals, and there are some sessions which could be combined with others, to make a longer tasting. However simple the food may be, I do stress the importance of quality ingredients. Better a sandwich of decent bread and butter with a filling of creamy farmhouse cheese or ham cut from the bone than a pretentious 'gourmet' meal where corners have been cut at every stage, so that flavours are never correctly developed and, even though the first sight of a dish may evoke the supposedly flattering 'It's just like a colour photograph!', the taste and consistency never please the discriminating palate. Indeed, beautiful though food can look, too much garnishing, especially by the unskilled, can never compensate for a lack of flavour; to put time and effort into this sort of would-be show-off cookery is as silly as deciding to buy a particular bottle of wine because it's got a pretty label – though, alas, many people do both!

If you are trying to show off your skill in cooking, always remember that it's the simple things, made perfectly, that can be far more impressive to people who really do know about such things. One superlative sweet dish does not need to be augmented by extras, such as creams, ices and complex pastries. One good, albeit modest and unusual wine will be of far more interest to the sincere wine lover than something expensive but second or third rate in terms of quality.

All the wines of the sessions have been tasted and drunk during the preparation of this book and all the suggested foods have certainly been eaten at various times, with enjoyment, not only by me but by friends who have considerable knowledge of food, cookery and wines. You need have no hesitation about sharing our experiences with your own friends.

GETTING DOWN TO THE SESSIONS –

THE STEPS IN TASTING

You've selected a couple of wines or more, you've decided what you're going to eat afterwards, you've taken the advice about glasses and opening bottles. Now you're going to taste!

The first step

Pour some wine into the glass. This, as you'll know by now, is a small quantity, a true 'tasting sample'. I calculate my helpings, when I pour these for myself, as two really small tasting mouthfuls. There must be sufficient in the glass to give you the chance of trying the wine twice, there shouldn't be so much that you can't swirl the wine around – for reasons which you'll understand in a minute. Explain, if necessary, that everyone will get a reasonable helping to drink later on.

Now you are going to taste the wine – but there are a few other activities involved too. You must look at the colour, sniff the smell, see what the flavour is like and, really important, see what your mouth feels like when you've swallowed the wine.

Don't think that any of this is going to take a long time or damp down any party spirit that should be generated when you and friends get together. But you are advised to devote a few minutes, as few as five or ten, to concentrating on the wine in your glass, before you start catching up with gossip or discussing anything else. If somebody prefers just to drink, let them. But, as a reader of this book, you'll be surprised and delighted by how much more enjoyable the wine will be when you do drink it, after having given it a little of your attention first. This is, after all, what the host should do as regards food and drink about to be offered to guests.

Whether you stand up or sit down while tasting is entirely for you to decide. Sometimes, if you're in a class studying wine, it's obviously necessary for you to be seated. However I admit that I find it difficult to taste when I'm sitting down and a well-known wine professor has decided that tests show that tasters remain relaxed, receptive and get tired less quickly if they stand to taste. One has the chance of moving about a little, of breathing to the bottom of one's lungs and there is no feeling of being cramped or confined to a small space.

This is another advantage about a short preliminary tasting before a meal – you can stand or sit, move about and make your notes if you wish without interfering with the arrangements.

The second step

Look at the wine. Whether it's red or white or pink, it should please you by its appearance. It should look 'alive'. Think of the difference in a glass of stale water, perhaps out of a carafe that hasn't been refilled for a day or more, side by side with a freshly poured glass of spring water. The one is dull, merely a liquid. The other, although colourless and without bubbles or texture, has something living about it. A wine's colour should be more interesting than a glass of liquid the same colour all the way through. The shades of colour and tone in a wine can be informative.

Check as to the 'brightness' of the wine. If it isn't quite clear and limpid, then make sure, before you criticise it, that you haven't poured too vigorously and churned up some slight deposit in the bottle, so that this impairs the clarity of the wine in your glass. But a few 'bits' aren't a cause for complaint – you may have pushed a few crumbs of cork down into the wine when you inserted the cork, you may have shaken up the bottle on the way home and not 'rested' it, so that the minute particles you didn't previously notice are 'in suspension' in the wine and now appear in the glass. Unless the whole look of the wine is dull and cloudy, there is nothing to worry about – but be more careful of the bottle next time.

In the various sessions, you'll find indications as to youth and age as evidenced by the colour, but in general remember that most dry white wines deepen in colour as they age – this applies to non-vintage as well as vintage wines – and that red wines, likewise, change colour, but they lighten, often having a slightly orange-tawny ring at the edge, where the wine meets the glass. Very young red wines are deepish red, varying, according to what they are, from almost black-purple to intense fuchsia-purple pinky red. Some are brilliant pink.

Some people hold a glass of wine up to the light to see the colour. But most find it easier to tilt the glass away from them, at an angle of 45°, holding it over something white. (Of course, I'm assuming that your sitting or dining-room isn't lit by several coloured bulbs making the overall light somewhat 'atmospheric'!) This is one reason why you don't need a full helping of wine in your glass for this stage of tasting. Tilt the glass and note how the pool of wine, whatever colour it is, will seem to have several 'rings' of tone as you hold it over the white paper or cloth or whatever. Some wines appear to have a veritable rainbow of different tones, shading outward to where the wine comes into contact with the glass. This outmost point is known as the 'miniscus' and it usually looks very pale, almost colourless. The deepest point of the wine in the middle of the pool is where the darkest colour will be. I always like the way in which someone who ran one of the great Bordeaux estates used to refer to this as the 'eye' of the wine – like the 'eye' of colour in a peacock's tail. Try, in registering colour, to differentiate between the mere 'white wine' and 'red' descriptions: there are many 'whites', just as, in the fashion world, there are many different 'blacks'. You may find it more difficult to describe a very pale white wine's colour, but try – is it in any way a bit like the colour of lemon juice? Or is it more golden, or straw in tone? With red wines, register whether the colour is 'red red' or whether it has a purple, even blue-black tinge, or whether there's the vividness of 'shocking pink' there.

Look, too, at the texture of the wine. Is it light and fluid, or does it seem to flow rather more slowly, as you move the glass around? A very sweet wine can look thick in texture. A sparkling wine, of course, has lots of bubbles – are these tiny, rising fast and furious, or do they rise only occasionally and slowly? All these things can tell you something – as the notes will indicate.

Turn the glass gently over the white surface in front of you and move the wine about. Different aspects of the wine's colour and texture may be revealed.

The third step

Now you're going to smell the wine. This is, for many people, the most important stage because it is the most revealing of what the wine is going to be like. 'Taste' in fact is very largely smell. You know how, when you have a bad cold, neither food nor drink have much flavour – you can't taste them.

All wine has or should have a smell. Some people find this rather shocking and prefer to use words such as 'bouquet' or 'aroma'. You will find examples of wines which demonstrate these two different smells later, and, if there's anything very wrong with a wine, it may have a definite stink, (see pp. 170 Enemies of wine), but all these words are terms to describe different smell impressions, which must always be wholly personal. You only have a small amount of wine in your tasting glass because you are now going to swirl the wine around in the bowl of the glass and, if you've filled the glass, you can't do this and will miss any smell – for which you've paid and which is part of the enjoyment of wine. This is why no wine lover will ever fill a glass by more than one-third or, possibly, half. The contact of the wine with the air is of great importance. Holding the glass by the stem, either steadying it on a table or simply holding it in the air, turn the wine around, smoothly and for several swirls. Then, at once, stick your nose into the bowl of the glass and sniff. The swirling of the wine aerates it and this releases and accentuates the elements that compose the smell; the incurving rim of the bowl of the glass directs this to your nose.

Take several little sniffs – you needn't sound as if you were having a session of inhaling. Take your nose out of the glass, swing the wine round once more and repeat the procedure. This should give you an idea of the smell of the wine in general. Do try to sniff so that the smell really does circulate around in the cavities within your face – if you can do this, far more definite impressions will be made by the various components of the overall smell.

A fine wine has a 'bouquet' – you'll discover this later on. But a certain type of wine may have an aroma – it will be 'aromatic', which one of the big dictionaries describes as 'having the distinctive flavour of a spice or a plant'. These two terms may help. You'll know what is meant by 'spicy' from experience in the kitchen. It may also help to know how the great man of wine who taught me defined the two: 'The aroma is, roughly speaking, the smell of the taste, whilst the bouquet is the impersonal collection of smells given off by the wine. The one (aroma) is projection, the other (bouquet) the very substance itself.'

People writing about wine and, I'm sure, those planning to write about it have compiled long lists of smells associated with different wines, some of which, I admit, mean nothing to me or else suggest something unpleasant! But smell is so personal and so difficult to describe that I suggest you put down whatever immediately comes into your mind as you sniff the wine – don't for an instant think what it *ought* to smell like, just register the first thing the smell suggests to you. It may be a surprising association, it may be something you've forgotten you ever registered as a smell – as when you sucked a lead pencil at school or sniffed chalk on a blackboard; it may be a milky smell, slightly sourish, it may be the smell that rises to your nose as you take out of your mouth the stone of an apricot or peach you've been eating, or the whiff of vanilla from some form of cosmetic cream. Try to capture this first impression, write it down if possible. It can be a wonderful aid to remembering and associating this particular wines with others. As Rudyard Kipling wrote, 'Smells are surer than sounds or sights to make your heart-strings crack.'

The fourth step

Now you're going to taste the wine. But not quite as if you were drinking it. Take a little time. Swirl it round in the glass then, as you bring the glass to your lips, take in only a very small amount of liquid and, along with it, a little air as well. There's no need to make a gargling noise, just *pull* the wine past your lips and make sure it is drawn over the inside of your mouth, over your tongue and gums and the soft flesh inside your cheeks. A number of wine authorities say one should actually chew a wine being tasted – so at least go partly through the motions! The wisp of air you draw in along with the wine will, like the swirling around, aerate it even more, sharpening up the effect it has, not only on the taste-buds, which are on your tongue, but the sensitive areas within the whole of your mouth.

Again, what does the wine feel like? What does it 'say' to you? Is it immediately pleasing, or do you receive a slight disappointment with the very first taste impression, which changes as you get used to the wine in your mouth? Does the wine seem to carry on the impression that was made by the smell – this consistency is important; but remember, too, that a wine can smell very fragrant, even sweet and yet be very dry when it gets into your mouth! Suppose you haven't been able to register much by way of smell – does the flavour make a more definite impression and, if so, of what? Does one particular element seem to predominate – have a look at pp. 55 for the components of wine – and can you pick out what the main taste or 'feel' is?

Go on trying the wine within your mouth for a few minutes, but don't try too hard to form an impression – as with many other activities, it's ideal to be alert but relaxed while you're tasting. Spit instead of swallowing if you wish.

Swallow. Then, after you've done so, breathe out through your mouth, giving a little 'huff'. This seems to whoosh all the past smells and flavours back again, sometimes giving a more precise impression than when you first put your nose into the glass. This 'after-taste' is worth noting, because sometimes it can indicate what a wine is going to be like when it develops further; if you feel that a particular wine is, as it were, holding itself back, then the after-taste may give you an idea of what it has in reserve, to demonstrate later.

That's all!

It takes far less time to taste than it does to read how to taste. Indeed, it's sense to taste rather quickly and make any notes at once. But what you should try to do, if you wish to study and taste wine, is to concentrate completely while you are tasting – even if this is for three or four minutes. You shouldn't worry about anything or anyone else at all. I know it can be difficult, especially for the host; but he or she can perhaps have a preliminary taste of the wines before guests arrive. Don't think of what you have previously heard about the wine – taste it as if you'd never tried it before. Don't pay any attention to the muttered comments of anyone else, or the expressions on their faces. You're the one who wants to find out about wine – and only if you devote all your attention and each one of the senses involved with tasting to it, just for those few instants, will you ever be able to form wise and helpful opinions about wine (and come to enjoy the company of those who also love and know it).

Stop tasting – and start eating and drinking. But don't forget, as you dine, to try to see how what you eat may change the first impressions of the wines you've been tasting. Usually they get better and better. But be honest and see whether, at the end of the meal, you agree. And, of course, whether you agree with the comments on the wines suggested, *that* will get you tasting and talking on your own!

P A R T 2

THE TASTING SESSIONS

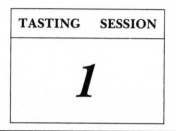

TASTING   SESSION

1

W	*I*	*N*	*E*	*S*

1 Liebfraumilch Blue Nun (H. Sichel & Sons), London
bottled
2 1980 Bulls Blood of Eger (Egri Bikavér), bottled by
Colman's of Norwich

Availability: Many retail outlets in the UK

Theme: The contribution of (a) dry white wines (b) red wines.

Practicalities: Cool the Blue Nun, either by putting the bottle
in a domestic refrigerator for an hour or a little longer – but
not more – or put it for fifteen minutes in a deep bucket of ice
and water, the level of the water coming up to the level of the
wine in the bottle. Draw the cork of the Bull's Blood about half
an hour before you are going to taste it, or, in cold weather, an
hour ahead of time.

What you're trying to do: There's a rôle for both white and
red table wines in any social drinking. What is the most
obvious contribution of either? Don't worry too much about
the details of the wines, although these are certainly interesting, but tackle this initial tasting so that you establish a few
basic procedures and get the idea of appraising wines. There
are no bad wines in the forthcoming selections – but in wine

as in many things 'you gets what you pays for' and quality doesn't come cheap, although with many of the bottles you'll sample it tends to be far in excess of the cost.

Remember that the aim of wine is to provide enjoyment, but people enjoy different things at different times. Some of the 'cleverer' commentators on wine enjoy criticising wines that have given many people pleasure – this is somewhat silly, because nobody can like all wines. Always go for the 'plus' properties of a wine. Most, however cheap, have something positive to contribute to the drinker. Here you are seriously tackling two wines that are world-famous and produced in vast quantities. Each has something to give you, whether or not you find yourself able to like it wholeheartedly; your natural inclination may be to white or to red, to dry or medium-dry, to full and fruity or to elegant and austere. But, as you taste, try to work out what the wine is trying to provide for you. Many skilled people and a lot of experience have been assembled in each bottle's contents. See whether you like it. If you do or if you don't, try to work out why,

Consult the book list if you need more detailed information, but, for the moment, simply *think* about the wines. Forget what they cost, what you may have heard about them, what someone who is supposed to know has said about them. If you wish, check again on the basic tasting routines given on pp. 62–69, but always form your own opinions – it's *you* and *your* likes and dislikes that matter.

Talking points: All Liebfraumilch is a 'quality wine' – there's the word 'qualitätswein' on the label. It's subject to specific controls. There are many different styles of Liebfraumilch (a comparative tasting of several would be an interesting exercise) and the maker of one wine may follow a different path, thinking of a certain type of customer. There are also the different grapes available to the makers and the different variations from year to year. Generalisations are tricky! Sichel's Blue Nun was evolved in the 1920s, during the terrible economic depression; it first hit export markets in the 1930s and, today, is the number one German wine in the world, acting as an introduction to German wines for millions of people. You won't find any Liebfraumilch widely listed in Germany, however – it's an ambassador abroad for German wines.

The Hungarian 'Egri Bikavér' or Bulls' Blood comes from the vineyards on volcanic soil around the town of Eger, where for centuries it has been made. The curvy baroque architecture of the delightful place is encircled by the impressive medieval walls. During an invasion by the Turks, the defending Hungarians sustained themselves with copious draughts of Egri Bikavér, brought up to them by the women of the town, themselves ready to fight side by side with the warriors. The red wine stained the beards of the Hungarians and the Turks, whose religion forbade them taking any alcoholic beverage, supposed the red liquid splashed down the faces and chests of their opponents to be something special, endowing them with heroic strength and courage, possibly from the local bulls – the bull being, as it is in many countries, the symbol of strength and prowess. Hence the name, Bulls' Blood. Anyway, the Turks were driven away – and the Hungarians have continued to enjoy Egri Bikavér ever since.

TASTING NOTES

Liebfraumilch Blue Nun

Several of the classic German wine grapes (Rheinriesling Müller-Thurgau, Sylvaner) contribute to the blend of this wine. But remember – in different years and when the wine comes from different regions it may be different in composition although, for a world-famous name such as this, the style will be followed to achieve consistency. This version comes from the Palatinate or Rheinpfalz region, where full-bodied white wines are made, that are suitable for partnering the sausages, cold cuts and cheeses of the area. Other permitted regions for Liebfraumilch are the Nahe, Rheingau and Rheinhessen.

The colour: White wine is of course never 'white' or colourless, although some can be only barely tinged with any tone. But young white wines from northern vineyards tend to be lighter in colour than those from warmer, southern areas and white wines deepen somewhat in tone with age. You will have to sort out your own colour 'tags' – lemon, lime, pale gold, medium gold, as you wish. Do bear in mind that a fairly definite golden tone doesn't necessarily mean that a white wine is sweet, nor that a very pale light lemon or grapefruit colour means that a white wine is dry. This one is pale lemon with a hint of gold at the heart of the wine when you examine it tilted away from you over something white so as to appraise any different bands of colour. This one hasn't much shading of this kind as it's young but don't suppose that any ageing would necessarily make it 'better'! It might darken in colour – and decline in the agreeable qualities with which it can please the drinker.

The smell: This is immediately obvious – it wafts up from the glass, eager to please the nose of the drinker and having a slightly full, enticing 'after smell'. The floweriness and somewhat fat, full smell you may notice (but don't say you do, unless you *truly do* – to accept a secondhand opinion from me will teach you little) may be due to the Müller-Thurgau grape in the blend. But smell this wine primarily thinking whether it pleases you – if it does, then try to work out why. If it doesn't, also try to work out why. Would you prefer something more aromatic – more scented – crisper – lighter? Register your opinion quickly – the longer you wait, the more complicated all these impressions become! – and go on to the next stage.

The flavour: When you take this wine into your mouth, it spreads out, making itself evident on tongue, gums, top and bottom and, although one doesn't taste with the teeth, seeming to be a liquid that has substance, almost so that you could try it between your upper and lower jaw for texture. This is important with wine – some wines are almost 'chewy' and others thin and you soon get the 'feel' of many. This wine is fairly full, but, as you drink or spit it, it passes from the palate seeming to get a bit lighter in texture. The last impression of the taste is of a wine that is fairly light and fresh, not wholly dry, but certainly not one that you could categorise as sweet.

Hungarian Bulls' Blood of Eger

The main grape used in this wine is the Hungarian Kadarka, but this is a native grape, although it is used in some other central European red wines. There is also a little Merlot in it, and this is a famous classic black grape; the Merlot is the one the vintagers eat when they want to quench their thirst, because, unlike most wine grapes, it's fruity and not too astringent to refresh the mouth. In the Bordeaux region the Merlot contributes a soft, very fragrant character to many of the great clarets (see Session 4) and it is grown in many parts of the world. Don't strain to detect this – never try to 'find' anything in a wine, no matter how eminent an authority tries to make you! If you can't pick out a particular characteristic, it's no tragedy; if you can or, more excitingly, if you can comment on something that even those eminent authorities may have not perceived, it's a triumph! (Although it doesn't necessarily mean that you're an 'instant expert'.)

This Bulls' Blood is ready to enjoy when bottled but, if you buy an extra bottle or two, you may find it rewarding to study the way 'bottle age' will change it slightly – whether you like this or not is up to you. Generally, it will lighten somewhat in colour and, if you've kept it properly (see p. 47), it may develop increased bouquet and a softness of flavour that can be very pleasing – or not, according to what you like in this type of wine.

The colour: A blueish-red, verging on the tone of a clove carnation or the darker variety of rhododendron. The wine does not display many bands of different colour tones, but at the rim, where it makes contact with the glass, it looks bluish-pink.

The smell: Fresh, clean and wholesome. A wine should always smell healthy, although give all the benefit of the doubt when first opened, as the tiny bit of stale air in the bottle may be unpleasant when you draw the cork and pour the wine at once. Here you have nothing complicated demanding your consideration – this is going to be a pleasant, easy to drink wine.

The flavour: Mouth-filling is the adjective – the wine laps all the areas of the mouth where you can register it. It comes in as an agreeable beverage. There's a light touch of acidity – a hint of crisp, fresh 'something', that makes it far more interesting than a red wine to quaff. As you swallow or spit, the mouth remains clean, pleased – you probably want to have another mouthful. As you 'huff' with your breath outwards, having tried the wine, there's a very slight final 'echo', which is the after-taste, which may remind you of raspberries, or some other soft fruit. There's nothing detailed to go on talking about here, in the boring way some wine snobs sometimes do. The wine is a straightforward, well-made, clean drink – old vintages of Bulls' Blood can be important red wines and make a contribution to the range of the world's reds. But here you have a good, honest, fairly young red, out to give pleasure and it does so. If you don't care for the type of pleasure it provides, try to work out why.

Conclusion: White wines should be lightly chilled so that their fragrance is accentuated, red wines benefit by being served not only at room temperature but by being opened and aired some time in advance of drinking. The appraisal of both is bound to be personal, but in general dry whites have a fresh, crisp contribution to make, reds a fruitiness and fullness.

Alternatives: There can't be any to this particular pair, but you could try the Liebfraumilch wines of other firms, plus the red wines of such central European countries as Romania, Yugoslavia, Bulgaria, if possible those that are made using some Merlot and any other classic grapes. Don't expect great and wondrous revelations – these are inexpensive wines for many occasions. But it's far harder to pick good 'cheapies' than the great names. And you should not think that it's necessary to write very detailed notes about a modestly-priced wine, which may only have a few pleasures to give you; it may be 'plain and simple' which is no bad thing, but be less complex than something rather more expensive that has a variety of attributes with which to please and challenge you.

Suggested food: Avocado pear, topped with finely chopped onion, salt, pepper, lemon juice and taramasalata, followed by goulash or cold game pie, and then apricot tart to follow. Less ambitiously, 'dips' of cream cheeses, some with paprika, onion, chives, aioli, green mayonnaise, with slivers of carrot, spring onion, peppers, cucumber, radishes and similar raw vegetables, with a cold ham or loin of pork with potato salad, followed by fresh fruit.

TASTING SESSION

2

1 Bereich Bernkastel
2 Bereich Nierstein, both of them from Langenbach
3 1981 Riesling d'Alsace, Gustav Lorentz of Bergheim

Availability: Threshers; Ashe & Nephew

Theme: Two wines to demonstrate the style of two German regions, plus an Alsace to show how admirable the Riesling grape can be.

Practicalities: All three wines should be chilled, so put them in the refrigerator for an hour or an hour and a quarter, or in a deep bucket of ice and water for about fifteen minutes. Draw the corks ten minutes before you try them – this will dissipate any 'bottle stink', the stale air in the bottle, which can sometimes initially affect light-bodied wines when the cork is first drawn. It will pass in a few minutes.

What you're aiming to do: The great German wines are wonderful, complex and delicate. The problem about the best, however, is that, especially if they verge on the special categories, and higher price ranges, they tend to be best enjoyed quite outside the context of a meal. But there are plenty of others that can be enjoyable with light dishes and these two admirably show off the regional style – the word 'Bereich' means area or district from which they come. There are probably several of the permitted grapes in both, including some Riesling in that of Bernkastel. The Alsace Riesling is a true Rheinriesling, like many of the finer German wines, but it not only comes from a different vineyard, it is essentially different in its characteristics and, like all Alsace wines, is excellent to drink even with quite robust dishes, such as some of the regional specialities. Don't even think of comparing Alsace wines with German wines – even though some (but not all) of the same grapes may be used to make them. Alsace is a fiercely independent region of France, even though West Germany is an appreciative customer for Alsace wines.

Talking points: We're traditional lovers of German wines, but far too often people try to accompany quite light inexpensive versions with fairly substantial British dishes – and the wine is really swamped. The advantage of Alsace wines is that they go well with a wide range of foods, from the fine and delicate fish and poultry dishes, to the abundant country fare featuring much pork, sausages and salads. People who never range outside the 'known names' of Germany will find two very pleasant wines to compare here, which may encourage sampling of wines of superior quality, perhaps just as refreshment between a few sympathetic wine lovers. As far as Alsace Riesling is concerned it's the Riesling that makes some of the finest wines of Germany, not, as you should be careful to remember, the 'Riesling' often seen on some of the good inexpensive wines of central Europe – this 'Riesling' will frequently be the variety known as 'Wälschriesling' or 'Olacsz Riesling', which isn't the same thing either as regards bouquet or flavour. It can be good and excellent value, but only the Rheinriesling can achieve greatness. For some people the Rheinriesling is the greatest white wine grape of all and there's a saying in Alsace: 'Riesling in the glass – heaven on earth!'

TASTING NOTES

In this, and some of the more straightforward sessions, there may be only one aspect of the wines stressed – although there may be many other points of interest.

Bereich Bernkastel

The Mosel-Saar-Ruwer region is very beautiful and the rivers wind tortuously, so that every tiny patch of vines will be slightly different from even those nearby, due to the curves and slopes being so varied. Bernkastel, with its twin town Kues across the Mosel, linked by a bridge, is one of the most picturesque, with a ruined castle on a crag towering above it, the vineyards sloping on every side and the black and white peaked roofed houses clustering along the river. Neither of these two wines is made from a single grape variety, so we're concentrating here on the regional style. But both wines are 'Quality wines', subject to controls.

The colour: A pale gold.

The smell: It has a cool, fresh whiff – wines from northern chilly vineyards are often very well endowed with fragrance.

The flavour: Agreeable, immediate fruitiness, a crisp, dry final impression lasting for quite a while after the wine has left the palate. This wine shows the fresh, charmingly fruity Mosel style, which is invariably appealing.

Bereich Nierstein

Nierstein is in the Rheinhessen region of Germany, beloved by many Victorian honeymooners because of its craggy, wild landscape. The dark reddish soil of many vineyards accounts for the usually fullish, slightly earthy character of some of the wines. If you went further south from Nierstein, you'd get into the Palatinate region (see Session 1) and, across the Rhine, at Worms, there's the headquarters of Langenbach, makers of both these wines. It's at Worms that the vineyard around the church of Our Lady (the Liebfrauenstift) probably gave the name 'Liebfraumilch' to certain wines – although this odd vineyard, right in the middle of the city, doesn't make Liebfraumilch as such today.

The colour: More golden in tone than the Bernkastel.

The smell: This has a full, almost fat fragrance, quite definite.

The flavour: This is a fullish, quite substantial wine, with a touch of fruitiness that reminds me of certain eating apples – perhaps a Worcester or a Russet – in the middle of the taste. It doesn't last as long in its final impression as the Mosel, but possibly has more impact in the first impression it makes on the palate.

1981 Riesling, Gustav Lorentz, Bergheim

Each of the wine growers in Alsace will make an individual wine, both because of their different house styles and because, along the picturesque 'Wine Road' that runs from north of Strasbourg down almost to Basle, there are many micro-climates – individual climatic conditions prevailing within even a small area. It is possible that the vintage of the wine will change by the time you read this – all to the good, however, because 1982 was an abundant year when good wines were made in quantity; 1983, although not making as much, was outstanding for quality at all ranges of the Alsace wines.

The colour: A mid to light gold.

The smell: Very pronounced – a waft of the Rheinriesling, which combines fruit and appeal with nobility. Note the allure of this fragrance, also the freshness.

The flavour: It slides onto the palate and expands – mouth-filling and full-bodied. Although there are many shades of taste in this wine, which is of moderately everyday quality, the finer and more expensive wines would have even more. This, with its balance of acidity and sweetness is definite in taste with a well-constructed 'shape'. This means that it has a beginning, a middle and an end, each aspect of it being in proportion. It trails away from the palate with definite charm. There's nothing aggressive about any aspect of it, but it makes a definite and firm impression on all the senses.

Conclusion: Regional variations make a tremendous difference to wines of delicacy, especially in areas where even small patches of vines may each contribute a different sort of wine to the overall product. Liebfraumilch is an overall introduction to German wine, but, if you are keen to explore further, you must sort out the different wine regions and register their character, then perhaps tackle the finer wines and register the different quality categories, many of which will be solely made from the Rheinriesling. The wonderful fragrance, which combines floweriness with a noble, impressive and complex bouquet, should be registered. Alsace is the wine that members of the wine trade will order when none of their own white wines feature on a list! It's always a bargain, it's infinitely variable in style, according to the maker and, of course, the quality category. More important, perhaps, is that it can partner most foods, including some quite substantial and highly flavoured dishes, including salads and every sort of sausage. The fragrance and mobility of the Riesling is obvious here too, but perhaps the grape in Alsace is rather less complex, except in the top quality categories.

Alternatives: You will be able to find regional German wines from other sources – if possible, get examples from the same establishment, which will be consistent in overall style and therefore stress the area differences. There are many good Rieslings from Alsace available in the UK, but these too will all be individual, according to the maker and also the exact region in Alsace where they originate and the vintage.

Suggested food: The centrepiece of the meal might well be a fine river fish – trout or, even, salmon trout, simply poached with a few boiled potatoes and maybe a lightly dressed green salad. You could start with little cream cheese pancakes, or possibly smoked eel – but go very easy on any horseradish sauce. A fruity sponge pudding or fruit tart with shortcrust pastry might conclude the meal. A more modest menu could simply consist of a fair selection of different cold meats, with a potato salad – choose a variety of sausages and salame, as well as cold pork, ham, salt beef and anything that makes an attractive selection from the delicatessen. Fruit can conclude this meal, but if you can extend your knowledge of cheese to the great Alsace cheese, Munster, so much the better – but it *is* admittedly a 'stinker' although not particularly strong in actual taste. If you offer various dips and meat pâté canapés as starters then why not attempt that superlative gutsy Alsace dish, a choucroute garni? This is pickled cabbage (you buy it made or in a can), 'garnished' with several sorts of sausage, smoked and fresh, plus chunks of bacon or gammon, pork chops or portions of cooked pork and, indeed, similar homely meats – with potatoes on the side. There are endless variations, but for the hearty appetites there could be meringues with fruit and cream to follow.

W   I   N   E   S

1 Austrian Grüner Veltliner
2 Italian Raboso del Veneto

Availability: Sainsbury's

Theme: Wines that are light, inexpensive and agreeable to drink with casual food can still illustrate the character of unfamiliar vineyard regions and unusual grapes, to interest even the experienced wine lover.

Practicalities: Chill the Grüner Veltliner for about an hour in the refrigerator or plunge it in a deep bucket of ice and water for fifteen minutes. Draw the cork of the Raboso half an hour before you are going to drink it.

What you're aiming to do: There are times when you want a wine that immediately pleases you and haven't the inclination to prepare more than casual refreshments – perhaps when people unexpectedly call or when you're planning an evening watching television and want food that's a little more sustaining than 'nibbles', but undemanding. The simplest sandwich, sausage roll or some cold cuts or a pizza brought from round the corner can be unbelievably enhanced by the appropriate bottle.

Talking points: The Grüner Veltliner is one of the most widely cultivated grapes in Austria. If you holiday there, you can enjoy it by the glass or carafe and its fresh character makes it particularly reviving if you drink it in a street side café after lots of sight-seeing. This 'Green Veltliner' can make fine estate wines too. The district of Krems, not far from Vienna, where this example originates, is in charming landscape, with bulging-towered country churches, trim houses, gardens of flowers as well as impeccably planted vineyards.

Raboso is a grape native to the Veneto region of Italy. The great authority, Burton Anderson, in his book 'Vino' says it is 'tasty in a robust way with an aroma of berries, herbs and earth.' The simple label term 'Vino da Tavola' (table wine) describes this wine exactly, enjoyable quaffing red. The picture on the label shows the great condottiero, or captain of mercenaries, Colleoni, which was sculpted by Verrocchio in 1488 and is considered one of the finest equestrian statues in the world. Colleoni, obviously a very tough character indeed, might have relished a long draught of Raboso when he got out of his hot armour and enjoyed sauntering in his native Venice.

TASTING NOTES

Grüner Veltliner

Made from a single grape, this wine is straightforward and intended to provide immediate pleasure.

The colour: Light to slightly medium straw in tone, without any noticeable shading. This is a young wine, intended for immediate consumption.

The smell: Pleasing, warm, ripe, enticing you to take a drink.

The flavour: A fairly substantial wine, that, unlike most, gives the drinker the impression of plunging in to fruit and certainly into juicy grapes. There's a firm inner taste, with a touch of warmth here as well, so that the wine isn't merely facile and superficial. But its aim is to please – which it does.

Raboso del Veneto

Remember this is from a fairly northern region of Italy, so the gutsy style of some Italian wines is, naturally, not over developed. The Raboso grape is somewhat high in both tannin and acid, attributes that are important in such classic wines as the red wines of Bordeaux (see Session 4) and many others, but here its individual style is much lighter, although you might compare notes with the Cabernet Franc of the Loire (Session 9) for some of its qualities.

The colour: Medium, rather soft-toned red, with a very slight touch of lightening at the edge. The wine is non-vintage and isn't intended for long-term maturation, but it has had sufficient age in bottle to be 'settled'.

The smell: This is light but definite and fragrant. There's an initial freshness, evocative of green leaves – perhaps a wood after a shower? Then there's an indication of fruit which is the final impression of the smell.

The flavour: This is a light-bodied wine – although this isn't to say that it's only of passing interest. It fills the mouth, without shoving itself at the palate and, towards the end, as you swallow it, there's a touch of firmness that then finishes definitely dry, refreshingly so. Although there's plenty of fruit here, the tannin is present via the dryness and the acidity is quite high, hence the crispness that stresses the fruity taste.

Conclusion: Both these wines come into the 'easy drinking' category and you might even find them 'good quaff' to use a wine drinker's bit of jargon. But they demonstrate two grapes of importance and, certainly if you travel in the regions where these are grown, you may find wines made from them that are both weightier and more complex. Meanwhile, they show how wines for almost anytime drinking can display individual interest.

Alternatives: If you can't find any Grüner Veltliner, then the Austrian Wachauer Schluck (the word means 'Gulp') may give you an idea of this sort of wine and it's widely available. The Raboso may be more difficult, unless you approach one of the specialist shippers (see p. 187), but otherwise you could opt for a Bardolino (see Session 7). Both the wines described here are multi-purpose and you could usefully have the Grüner Veltliner for an anytime drink, the Raboso for an anytime partner to sandwiches – the good sandwich is never to be despised and remember, there should always be more filling than bread!

W   I   N   E   S

1 Château Loudenne blanc, 1983
2 Château Loudenne rouge, 1982
3 Château Loupiac Guadiet
  all château bottled

Availability: Peter Dominic

Theme: An introduction to the wines of Bordeaux, white and red, dry and sweet.

What you're aiming to do: Although some of the greatest and most costly wines in the world come from the Bordeaux region, there are plenty of others within the purse range of most of us. The red wines are always made from a blend of grapes, but it is the Cabernet Sauvignon that is the blackbone of all claret. But that wine is rather specially made! If used alone, the astringent wine the Cabernet usually makes can seem dry or stalky, which is why certain other black grapes are used as well. These include the Cabernet Franc (see Session 15) and the Merlot. The Sauvignon Blanc gives the fresh, 'green' smell to the dry whites (see also Session 8) and it is sometimes used on its own in this region. But it also contributes to the firmness of the sweeter white wines, where the Sémillon bestows oftness and fragrance as the 'noble rot' develops (see Session 6). It's relevant here to say something about people who assert that they know nothing about wine but 'can tell claret from Burgundy'. Of course, ideally, one should be able to do so – claret is made from several grapes, Burgundy from one only. But even the greatest authorities have been mistaken – or caught out; in certain years and with wines made in certain ways the two great reds can be confused.

Practicalities: Put the two white wines in the refrigerator an hour ahead of time and, when you take out the dry white, leave the sweet white there until you're ready to drink it. Or, if this is easier, plunge both wines into a bucket of ice and water and leave the sweet wine there when you take out the dry one. Draw the cork of the red wine at least an hour ahead of drinking time, or decant it into a decanter or carafe an hour ahead.

Talking points: Here there's a dry white – don't believe people who tell you that all white Bordeaux is sweet! – plus a red, and a delicately sweet white. The first two come from the famous property Château Loudenne (the sweet white is made elsewhere but selected by the Loudenne authorities) which, in 1875, was bought by the Gilbey Brothers, who created a great establishment in France as well as in Britain. Today, the estate and its vast cellars belong to International Distillers & Vintners (IDV for short) whose retail chain is Peter Dominic.

The wines of Bordeaux, an area that was owned by the English for 299 years, are in many ways the standard by which white and red wines are appraised throughout the world. Here you have the baby wines, but they too show why claret – red Bordeaux – and the luscious sweet whites have become renowned. The dry whites in recent years have, thanks to modern methods of making and keeping, become fresh, zippy and very easy drinking. Whether you like Bordeaux wines or can't easily enjoy all of them, you can't ignore them – they are among the classics although, of course, there are infinite variations of style and quality among them.

TASTING NOTES

Ch. Loudenne Blanc 1983

With these classic wines, you should note the appellation contrôlée or A.C. or A.O.C.; this, in full, 'is appellation d'origine contrôlée' and signifies exactly where the wine comes from. There are (see pp. 25) A.C.s and A.C.s, some fitting inside each other; usually, the more detailed the A.C. the more specific the area. This wine is A.C. Bordeaux – it is controlled as regards where it comes from, the grapes and the way they are cultivated (the grapes are a blend of Sauvignon Blanc and Sémillon) and the minimum degree of alcohol in the wine. Note the picture of Ch. Loudenne on the label. The rose-pink house, of a single storey except for its towers, has the vineyard running right up to the terrace.

The colour: Pale but a definite gold.

The smell: This wine comes from a fairly warm vineyard (else the great black grapes wouldn't ripen to their best), but it's been very correctly made to suit the taste for dry white wines. You certainly won't find it as crisp as, say, a Muscadet (see Session 6), but it is dry. There's a touch of clean standing water in the smell – if you're lucky enough to know someone with a swimming pool in the open under a tree, there's a special freshness about the smell of the water, which I pick up here. The white Sauvignon grape gives the freshness, others of the permitted Bordeaux grapes provide fullness and a touch of softness.

The flavour: This is definitely a dry wine, but it's been made trimly cool and fresh – old-style white Bordeaux wines could be a bit frumpish, rather like ladies who have let their figures get quite out of control! Here we have a direct taste, plus a very slight touch of fat. It ends with a fairly definite full impression on the palate.

Ch. Loudenne 1982

This red wine shows off the various Bordeaux grapes – you'll study the Cabernet Sauvignon in more depth in (Session 14), but along with this there's the contributions of the other claret grapes, the Cabernet Franc (for zest and crisp fruitiness) and a little soft sweetness from the Merlot grape. The A.O.C. is 'Médoc' and Loudenne is situated on the Gironde estuary, near the tip of the long pointed tongue of the Médoc that licks up into the Atlantic. It's not uncommon for both red and white wines to be made at Bordeaux estates, but it is unusual for the quality of both to be virtually equal, as happens at Loudenne, although the white Loudenne is, naturally, a wine to be drunk young and fresh, whereas the red wine can last and, in certain vintages, develop most agreeably and rewardingly.

The colour: The sample when I tasted it was very dark – red Bordeaux is deep purple red, not, however, black in tone. Note the different colour shades – always evident in good Bordeaux.

The smell: Very much the Cabernet Sauvignon 'leaves and vegetation' smell!. It's fresh, quite assertive and some might say that there's almost a whiff of chocolate or vanilla about it. You are not immediately invited to taste the wine, but there it is, saying, 'I'm moderately important', therefore suggesting you do taste it.

The flavour: Very firm – 1982 was a ripe, fine vintage. Here you have a 'baby' claret showing its quality. The tannin (the element that 'pulls' the mouth) ensures it of a fairly long life, the fruit is obvious, balanced by the underlying crispness of the acidity. It's reasonable to say that you may decide you don't find it easy to like red Bordeaux wines. Fair enough, but so many people have found them the most rewarding drinks and fascinating wines to talk about that you should at least try to see why and, if they are not as yet for you, come back and try them in the future. Do bear in mind that this is the sort of wine that is quite difficult to appraise apart from food – although the food can be very simple and plain. On an empty stomach clarets can seem a bit tough, but take a biscuit and see what they then say to you – they have perhaps more than any other wine an appeal to the mind as well as the senses.

Ch. Loupiac Gaudiet 1978

This is an A.C. 'Loupiac' – a region that is 'across the river', by which is meant the Garonne, and that is on the opposite side to the great sweet white wine regions of Sauternes and Barsac. But these 'baby' sweet whites (red and dry whites are also made here) have much to give in terms of pleasure – the Loupiac wines have, to me, always an odd flick of dryness as they leave the palate, making them akin to the Barsacs. In the region you may well get offered such wines as apéritifs or even with oysters or foie gras at the start of a meal – once you've got over the rather odd feeling that 'It's sweet – is it right?'

you'll probably thoroughly enjoy the experience. Such wines are still very reasonably priced, too.

The colour: A definite straightforward light gold. Golden wines are not all sweet – but this one has sweetness at its heart.

The smell: A clean, breezy aroma, with plenty of push behind it. This is a wine from a warm vineyard (and a warm vintage if you get this sample), but it's prettily vigorous and quite neat in smell.

The flavour: There's a fullness, with the dryness of the Sauvignon Blanc (see Session 8) in conjunction with the Sémillon, which last-named grape provides the warm, alluring taste. You do have a touch of the 'noble rot' smell and taste (Session 6) which, in the Bordeaux vineyard, can be contributory to a luscious wine. This one is somewhat of a soubrette – a very charming drink, to sip and appraise, registering the sweet Bordeaux style.

Conclusion: Dry white Bordeaux can be straightforward, clean and of immediate quality. The red wines are so varied that generalisations are risky – but they can be complex, appealing to the mind as well as the senses, not always easy to enjoy except with food, but most interesting. The sweet white wines can be enjoyed even between meals as a cool refreshment, but are particularly delightful partnering a fruit-based pudding or gâteau. In fact, in the region they are even sometimes served with a first course of oysters accompanied by the small garlic-flavoured sausages of the area or indeed with foie gras, but this really is a bit overwhelming for many people! A very sweet wine early in the meal or more than a small glass beforehand can cut the appetite.

Alternatives: You can certainly find a small-scale red Bordeaux at most wine shops. As vintages can vary a great deal here, it's been impossible to generalise, but with a 'little' wine you can choose a fairly recent light vintage – though try to get some advice about this if possible. The dry white wines are also fairly generally on sale; these days an Entre-Deux-Mers needn't be very sweet. The sweet wines are also well distributed; if you can't get a Loupiac, then a 'baby' or ordinary

Barsac will probably be more in accordance with this selection than a Sauternes, because Barsacs end with an odd 'flick' of dryness whereas Sauternes are luscious from start to finish.

Suggested food: The meat most lovers of Bordeaux would choose might well be lamb – the local lamb is famous. But you could have any roast or grilled meat. The first course, following local traditions, might be a platter of shellfish, or simply shrimps and prawns. Have lemon juice instead of mayonnaise with the light dry white wine and remember to use your left hand to squeeze the lemon, so that you don't have a lemony hand round your glass, detracting from the smell when you drink! With the lamb, go very easy on any mint sauce or, preferably, have redcurrant jelly. French dessert fruit, macaroons, or a syllabub or creamy pudding made with some of the sweet wine can conclude a rather special meal. More economically, a casserole of lamb or even Irish stew or a veal pie, hot or cold may be served, prefaced by avocados with a very light dressing, and some fresh fruit to finish. More simply still, you could have the dry white wine as an apéritif and then a cold chicken or turkey pie, possibly with baked potatoes or simply a selection of cheeses instead of any meat, followed by some good eating apples – do a tasting of different ones to keep up the interest!

1 Vinho verde (branco)

Availability: Marks and Spencer

Theme: A unique wine, formerly local, now known every-where showing the sort of wine that is needed to stand up to difficult foods.

Practicalities: Serve cool – chill in the refrigerator for an hour or plunge into a deep bucket of ice and water for ten to fifteen minutes. If you're really in a hurry, put your wine glasses in the fridge as well – they'll look pearly when you pour the wine into them.

What you're aiming to do: There are times when you can't prepare anything elaborate for a meal, even when you've invited people back or know friends are probably going to drop in. This is when a bottle of wine can make all the difference – especially if it's suitably chosen. Of course there are plenty of wines that can make all the difference to a take-away meal, you'll find many in the various sessions, but vinho verde is both interesting in itself and excellent for accompanying foods that can be a bit taxing to delicate wines. Although vinho verde is widely available, it's an interesting wine and people don't know all that much about it as yet, so the choice of such a wine for an impromptu meal, (it could be cheese and tomato sandwiches, pizza, or chicken in the basket) is a deft way of showing those who share it with you that wine is the supreme convenience food. (And you will find it can dress up many of the domestic remnants you eat up en famille.)

Talking points: Vinho verde is, in Portuguese, 'green' wine. But this doesn't refer to the colour. Indeed, more red vinho verde is made than white. This is an odd wine, which many people can't easily enjoy, although in Portugal vast amounts are quaffed with the hundreds of smoked cod recipes the locals make. (Yes, red wine with fish, and the acidity of the red vinho verde can be delightful with bacalhão, smoked cod, something evolved by the adventurous Portuguese fishermen venturing far from home for their catch.) No rosé wine is a vinho verde, although many otherwise good reference books tell you it is – but legally it can't be! Look for the special paper seal on the bottle of each vinho verde.

This 'green' wine comes from the north of Portugal, where, in a region called the Minho, the vines are trained high. Indeed, pickers of the grapes at vintage time have to climb ladders and, in some plots, the vines twine themselves up trees, posts, anything high. This particular method of growing means that the grapes are high in acidity, hence very fresh and crisp wine is made, which is 'green', and at its most enjoyable while young. The wine has a slight fizz. (This is due to the grapes receiving less reflected sunlight from the ground and so they contain less grape sugar.) The wine is still tending to 'work', that is why the mini-fizz of a part of its fermentation is still apparent and it shouldn't be kept for long or it will lose its freshness. Several Portuguese grapes are involved and it's to the credit of the Portuguese that they've never attempted to draw comparisons with the other classic wines by compromising with well-known names – indeed, there's no possible 'other' name for a vinho verde except you can call it 'pétillant', which means very slightly sparkling.

In former times, each establishment making the wine would simply bottle it when ready – notice the seal on the back of this bottle and the address of a well-known firm in Gaia, the entrepôt or wine centre opposite Oporto. But of course customers want continuity of style and therefore the tiny bubbles of the gas in the wine are now adjusted so that each firm's vinho verde is made to a quality standard. Even so, they are all individual – one vinho verde may be less fizzy than another. The same applies to the dryness.

Vinho verde is a wine to enjoy on many occasions and for immediate pleasure. It's not too serious, it should be good. Its versatility is considerable.

The colour: Light golden tone, although it is still reminiscent of lemon. The bubbles are tiny, but they go on rising even after the bottle is open and the wine poured – this is a sign of a well-made pétillant wine.

The smell: Fruity – it reminds me of a very good grapefruit! But there's the indication of fresh, cool vineyards, no interfering smell.

The flavour: Fuller than many vinhos verdes, the fizz quite frothy initially, then the wine settles down to be fairly fruity, dry but quite full. One might use the adjective 'buxom', because it's capable of accompanying quite fatty foods and sauces.

Conclusion: This is a particularly 'local' Portuguese wine that has now acquired a place in export markets because its freshness, mini-fizz and light style make it admirable for many occasions of contemporary wine drinking. Yet it retains its special and unusual local style, slightly adapting the truly shrill dryness of the region's wine to a fuller character, suited to people who like a little more full-bodied wine for some occasions. It's not to be considered too seriously – it's a wine to quaff with pleasure, not to think about for very long – but a good vinho verde plays an important part in the contemporary drinking scene.

Alternatives: There aren't any! But you could try a pétillant wine from other regions, although it will be totally different. Cyprus Bellapais is a white, slightly pétillant good wine, also the Apremont from Savoy (Session10) or any wine that's described on its label as 'pétillant', although of course it won't be the same. However, as white vinho verde is so widely stocked in the UK you shouldn't have problems if you can't find this one; bear in mind that it doesn't *always* come in the dumpy, flagon-shaped bottle. Nearly all the big retail chains have their own vinho verde branco (white) and each will have its own particular style. But the general remarks here apply to them all.

Suggested food: As has been indicated, this is an anytime drink, because of its crisp, fresh style and because it isn't too full to be only a wine to partner food. It would easily partner Chinese take-away, chicken in the basket, pizza, cheese and tomato sandwiches, or you could use it as an accompaniment to any seafood or shellfish picnic – if you go to the coast and revel in winkles, cockles, mussels, shrimps and even oysters. But where it is most useful is for that otherwise very 'difficult' food, smoked salmon, which swamps fine and delicate wines. So, whether you're able to serve a few wafer slices with brown bread and butter, or buy 'pieces' to mince and make into sandwiches, or use for a superb kedgeree as a supper dish, vinho verde will be excellent. You can serve it with piquant canapés – stuffed eggs, anchovy toasts, dips of strong cheese, say before any formal meal. Finally, if you want to make an unusual 'mix', try vinho verde with a small teaspoonful of cassis (blackcurrant) liqueur in each glass, stirred up. This is a gorgeous variation on 'vin blanc cassis' (white wine with cassis), now so chic and, although the cassis isn't cheap (blackcurrant syrup really won't substitute), the amount used for each portion is small, so the drink isn't too extravagant.

W	*I*	*N*	*E*	*S*

1 Muscadet de Sèvre et Maine
2 1974 Dão, Região de Marcada
3 Monbazillac

Availability: Sainsbury's

Theme: Learning to tell the difference between wines from cool, hot and cold, and temperate vineyards and buying another example of a wine which demonstrates noble rot.

Practicalities: Chill the Muscadet and the Monbazillac for an hour in the refrigerator or put both into a bucket of ice and water fifteen minutes before the Muscadet is to be opened. Leave the Monbazillac in the fridge or iced water until you need it. If possible, draw the corks on both wines ahead of time (ten minutes or so) and then replace them lightly. Open the Dão one or two hours ahead of time and leave the cork out. Put the bottle in the room where you are going to eat.

What you're aiming to do: It's often possible, when tasting, to see whether a wine is the product of a cool or even cold vineyard or a sunbaked hot one. It's more difficult when the vineyard has a temperate climate. The three wines are all typical of their areas, although the Dão region is inclined to be cold and wet in the winter and hot in the summer. This group of wines would go with most conventional three course meals. If you wish to omit one, leave out the Monbazillac, unless you really do enjoy a definitely sweet wine – it may be a bit too sweet for some people to serve by way of apéritif or with a first course but if you omit the Muscadet, you can try this.

Talking points: The Muscadet region, at the sea end of the River Loire – the longest river in France – is undulating countryside, with grey châteaux, the elegant town of Nantes and a proud wine tradition. The Muscadet grape is nothing whatsoever to do with the Muscat or Muscatel grapes – in fact it originally came from Burgundy, where it was called the 'Melon'. For long it was merely a local wine but, thanks to modern wine making methods, it now appeals widely and, especially with the fish and shellfish of the region, it's a delicious crisp accompaniment to any dish with mayonnaise.

Dão, in the rocky region of central Portugal, is a vineyard that's often based on granite – the locals refer to this 'bleeding into the wine'. Remember that the great port vineyards are granitic. Pine forests make the air aromatic, and, in the summer, the mountain sides are multi-coloured with market gardens. But the winter can be bitingly cold and wet and the locals need to be tough. White wines are also made but the warm-hearted reds are yet one more taste we share in common with the Portuguese – our 'oldest ally', since a treaty signed between England and Portugal in 1373. Three Portuguese grapes contribute to this Dão.

Monbazillac comes from the Bergerac region in south-west France. It's white and sweet in a rather special way – being produced by the action of a special fungus on individual grapes. This curious phenomenon is known in Latin as *Botrytis cinerea* or 'noble rot', because it seems as if it shrivels the fully ripe grapes (they look almost fuzzy) so that they contain minute drops of luscious juice. Botrytis wines are famous (and expensive) throughout the world and the greatest German sweet wines and the fine Sauternes are all made by the 'noble rot' in action. (You'll note a botrytis wine from Bordeaux in Session 4.)

TASTING NOTES

Muscadet de Sèvre et Maine

The Sèvre et Maine region is associated with the best Muscadet wines. In the summer the Muscadet countryside is charming – but it certainly can rain and be chilly in the winter, when the Atlantic storms arrive.

The colour: Light and pale, as is usual in white wines from cool vineyards, although they may turn more golden when old. This one has a slight tinge of gold to the overall fresh yellow tone.

The smell: This definitely smells cool and fresh – think of the pleasant freshness of wet flagstones after a shower. The wine is made from ripe grapes – but can you feel the touch of chilliness behind the pleasant smell that signals the coolness of the vineyard?

The flavour: This is very full and substantial. Some Muscadets may seem thin and very high in acid, which is not necessarily bad (in certain years and with certain wines), but this style may not appeal to you. This example, however, is quite plump, if you think of it in terms of somebody's silhouette. Note that the wine leaves the mouth feeling refreshed and giving the definite impression of being dry.

1974 Dão

The Dão wines are capable of improving with bottle age. They represent enormous value, as they are so suitable for many dishes that can overwhelm some good wines.

The colour: Tilt the glass away from you over something white and note the definite bands of shading from the pool in the centre up to where the wine touches the glass. There are several shades and the wine is dark, deep crimson at its deepest point, lightening to a tawny rim – almost the orange tone of a robin's breast. This indicates the age. Age is not invariably a good thing in a wine, because some wines are much better when young and fresh, but a very young Dão would be tough and almost 'chewy'. Like the Englishman of the song, it 'needs time' and here it has it. The trails down the side of the glass indicate the glycerine content – an element that should be present, though not to excess, and that can contribute roundess or smoothness.

The smell: This wafts warmth of a compact, intense sort up to your nose. The sun has baked these vineyards, but, behind this warmth, there's a sensation of firm, almost austere character – that's the contribution of the cold and the granite. Some of the great red Rhône wines might remind you of this one.

The flavour: Very definite – firm, plenty of taste to enjoy with an inner flavour that, as you pull the wine around in your mouth, can perhaps suggest rocks and stones or merely make you decide that it's 'big', which it is. There is a generous, welcoming taste overall but, as the wine leaves the palate and the fruitiness fades, you'll have an impression of a wine with a very definite 'constitution', like a well-built and well-proportioned person.

Monbazillac

The fragrance of this wine takes a few minutes to come up from the glass, so, when you're ready, take the cork out again and pour in good time, twirling the wine round in the glass to aerate it a bit.

The colour: Clean, bright yellow. It is not true that all sweet wines are deep gold, nor that all dry wines are very pale in tone – but there is a slight truth in both these generalisations.

The smell: Note this, because it does indicate the action of the 'noble rot', although you may at first only appreciate this by finding the wine somehow very intense, with a compact scent. Several grapes contribute to Monbazillac, the Sauvignon Blanc, Sémillon and Muscadelle also being used for the great white Bordeaux wines. The Sémillon provides that alluring fragrance, the Muscadelle the very obvious ripe quality, while the Sauvignon – which you'll find makes fine dry whites (see Sessions 4 and 8) holds the two together, in balance.

The flavour: This is a direct wine, moderately sweet, with a clean final impression, never cloying. You can serve it after the Muscadet, if you want an all white wine meal or, if you're having a fruity first course, it could go with this instead of the Muscadet. Or you might enjoy it with fresh ripe fruit in the garden, outside the context of a meal.

Conclusion: Cool vineyards tend to make wines that can have pronounced fragrance, even if they are light in overall style – which, remember, has nothing to do with alcoholic strength! Heat by itself can make rather 'obvious' wines, but cold winters and certain soils, such as the granite in the Dão area, can give the wines character and firmness. The 'noble rot' wines vary enormously in weight and, of course, according to their grapes and regions, but, if you get used to trying different ones, you will be able to pick out this distinctive fragrance and concentration of flavour, which differentiates them from wines that are merely and straightforwardly sweet.

Alternatives: You should be able to get Muscadet from most retailers – although remember that each will have an individuality and not necessarily bear more than a family resemblance to this one. You can also find château Muscadets from some outlets, which will be even more individual. Dão is also generally available, although from different makers and probably of different vintages, but if you can't find it, then a Côtes du Rhône red would be an optional choice – but this really is a different type of 'sunbaked but savage' climate wine. Monbazillac, becoming popular once again, may be less easy to discover, although some very fine wines do get listed; try an inexpensive Sauternes as a possible second choice.

Suggested food: Platter of seafood and crustacea, with mayonnaise, or prawn cocktail; steak, kidney and mushroom pie, or Irish stew; fresh fruit salad – with some Monbazillac included. Or, more simply, you could serve cold fried fish with tartare sauce or simply a squeeze of lemon (the Muscadet will stand up to this) followed by some matured English cheeses; they are too strong for many red wines, but not for Dão. The Monbazillac can be sipped with shortbread or plain sponge cake afterwards.

W   I   N   E   S

1 Verdicchio
2 Bardolino
3 Lambrusco rosso

Availability: Sainsbury's

Theme: Learning how to complement rich dishes with appropriate wines – here all wines from Italy.

Practicalities: The Verdicchio and the Lambrusco should be served cool or, in stuffy weather, definitely cold, so put the bottles in the refrigerator for an hour or plunge them into a deep bucket of ice and water for fifteen minutes. The Bardolino can be served at room temperature, like other red wines, but, in the summer, you may find its delicious fruitiness enhanced if you cool it slightly, to the temperature at which it might come from the cellar.

What you're aiming to do: Some Italian wines, such as Chianti, are very well known, others less so, even when extremely adaptable to both fine cooking and informal foods. Remember that it's a safe guideline that a wine should either complement or contrast with a dish, so, with very rich things, a crisp, fruity wine may be quite as acceptable as a rich, impressive one. The fruit sauces – gooseberries with mackerel, redcurrant jelly with lamb, orange with duck, apple sauce with pork – are well-known accompaniments. But in wine regions certain fruity wines perform the same rôle.

Talking points: Wine-rich Italy is able to enjoy thousands of wines and, often to the surprise of the tourist, doesn't usually bother about conventional partnerships of white wine with fish, red with roasts and grills. You drink what you enjoy! The most unusual wine in this selection is Lambrusco, which is a run-away success in the USA where its fruity, slightly fizzy style is popular at the poolside or for buffet parties. In its homeland, however, it's traditional with zampone, the stuffed pigs' feet of Emilia-Romagna, where the historic city of Bologna is not nicknamed 'The fat' for nothing, as it abounds in first-rate restaurants of all categories.

There are two things to bear in mind when tasting Italian wines: they can make great wines, but they tend to concentrate on making pleasing wines to be drunk with food – and, generally, they do not stress the importance of a wine's bouquet or fragrance as much as those of us in more northern regions. So don't mark down an Italian wine for lacking this aspect, and do appreciate that it can probably be enjoyed with meat, fish, cheese, poultry or by itself – even if it's red!

Verdicchio: the 'Verde' bit of its name indicates the green freshness that's typical. This is a wine from the Marche region, halfway up the Adriatic coast of Italy. The Verdicchio vine is native to Italy and it has been making wine at least since the fifth century A.D. Only fairly recently has Verdicchio become widely known, at least partly because of the 'amphora' shaped bottle, like the clay vessels that the ancients used to keep cool in the earth. It's a wine to be drunk young and when at its freshest. You can also enjoy it as a 'spumanti' or sparkling wine – this example is semi-fizzy.

Bardolino comes from the north-east of Italy, where the delightful lake resorts (Garda being the most famous) are flanked by many vineyards. Verona is in this area as are the delightful wine towns Soave and Valpelicella. Lambrusco is from Emilia-Romagna, the northern wine region that straddles east to west, with Modena its centre, and Bologna where gastronomes flock to eat.

TASTING NOTES

Verdicchio

A wide range of red as well as white wines are made in the region. Verdicchio, as has been said, is a local grape, but two other classic white wine grapes can be included. The term

'Castelli de Jesi' refers to the castles (castelli) that surround the historic old town of Jesi.

The colour: Pale, barely lemon-yellow, with an indication or touch of fizziness in the tiny bubbles that will be seen fastening themselves to the side of the glass.

The smell: Very light, but fresh and clean. My own tasting notes often mention 'cold tiles' because this clean, slightly stimulating cool aroma does to me evoke the smell you notice when you've washed down ceramic tiles in the kitchen or wiped a bathroom wall with plain hot water.

The flavour: The little 'liveliness' that is the fizz in the wine pushes along the taste. This is a neat, dry wine, straightforward, leaving the palate toned up.

Bardolino

The Veneto doesn't only mean 'Venice' and a huge range of wines is made in this region. There are mass producers and individual makers of fine and costly wines, some using local, some classic wine grapes. Bardolino, a delightful place on Lake Garda, makes red and rosé wines, served in their birthplace at cool cellar temperature in summer. A mixture of grapes, peculiar to the region, are used.

The colour: Brilliant pinky-red, particularly attractive and typical of Bardolino.

The smell: Fresh, light, indicating fruitiness, uncomplicated.

The flavour: Also light and fruity – the smell leads on to the taste. The crispness is very welcome if you're eating anything fatty. It's a 'quaffing' wine in that you want to drink more – and it leaves the palate fresh.

Lambrusco

Made from a grape of the same name, with a long list of different sub-varieties, of which the Grasparossa is possibly the best known. It can be dry or sweetish, as is this sample, and the touch of bubbliness (different from that in the Verdicchio) is natural in the wine. Opinions are fiercely divided – is it just a 'pop' wine, or one of the individual specialties of the area?

Note, in this sample, the low alcoholic strength, which makes it undemanding drinking.

The colour: A definite purplish pink, the colour of the darker outer petals of a fuchsia – very pretty.

The smell: A light, vaguely fruity fragrance, wholly pleasant.

The flavour: Pronounced fruit – mouth-filling. My own notes with this wine invariably ring variations on 'Raspberries' 'Raspberry and redcurrant', 'Raspberry jam', with a zingy freshness given by the slight effervescence. Because this is such an odd wine to many drinkers, it's fair to give it a bit more attention – those who like it, love it, those who don't, possibly scorn it. But the locals in Emilia-Romagna quaff it copiously and there are many parts it can play in entertaining.

Conclusion: Italian wines aren't just Chianti and Soave! And it's worth noting that they aim at providing a slightly different pleasure from many French wines. They can be served with a huge range of foods and are mostly robust enough to enable the white wine lover to drink white through the meal, the red wine drinker to partner reds with the most highly seasoned fishes. Look for the direct style and remember the follow-on of flavours, which can compensate for the somewhat subdued bouquet of many Italian wines. (After all, for formal occasions, many Italians will drink a vermouth or one of their sparkling wines (see p. 163 by way of apéritif.)

Alternatives: Verdicchio is quite widely available, likewise Bardolino, and Lambrusco is increasingly popular. If you wish, serve the Lambrusco with a first course, or even as an apéritif, or, for a buffet meal, you can drink it throughout. There are specialists in Italian wines (see p. 189), but remember, if you choose wines from them, they may not, even if they bear the same names, bear more than a general resemblance to those described here, but have greater individuality.

Suggested food: If you want an all Italian meal, I suggest: zampone (if you can get it from an Italian delicatessen), which is traditional with Lambrusco; then vitello tonnato with the Bardolino. Serve the Verdicchio as an apéritif with olives (black) and little chunks of Parmesan cheese. Later, serve the

Lambrusco with any fruit dish, such as melon filled with assorted fresh fruits or peaches. For a British menu, try a kipper pâté with the Verdicchio, roast pork with the Bardolino and summer pudding or peach meringue pie with the Lambrusco. Or, more simply, you might have a huge dish of spaghetti with a Bolognese sauce (of the region for Lambrusco), and nibble slivers of coppa (raw ham) with the apéritif, and after any Italian cheese to finish the red wine, offer pears cooked in red wine.

W	I	N	E	S

1 Chenin, Rémy Pannier
2 Sancerre, 1983, Patient Cottat
3 Cabernet de Touraine 1982, Cuvée Prestige
4 Château du Breuil 1983, Côteaux du Layon.

Availability: Oddbins

Theme: Some Loire wines, each from a single classic wine grape: Chenin Blanc, Sauvignon, Cabernet Franc.

Practicalities: All these wines (yes, including the red wine!) should be served cool, but, as the label of the Sancerre says, 'Cool, not iced'. If it's a cold day, however, the Cabernet de Touraine can be served at room temperature. If you put all the wines in the refrigerator for an hour or a deep bucket of ice and water for fifteen minutes, then they will be ready to serve; the Coteaux du Layon, being the sweetest, is served last and needs to be the coldest.

Note: if you wish to serve all white wines, simply omit the Cabernet. If you want to cut down on one wine, serve the Sancerre as an apéritif and with any first course. If you truly can't enjoy crisp dry wines, then skip this session, because all these wines, except the last, are definitely dry or dryish.

What you're aiming to do: You already probably know Muscadet, from the sea end of the Loire and made from the grape of the same name (see Session 6). Here are three more important classic wine grapes to register, via wines that make easy drinking and have proud histories. These examples are small-scale and, therefore, inexpensive. You can find wines from the same grapes, many from individual estates, probably available only in smallish quantities because of the limited production, that can cost you twice or three times the price of these. So this is a good tasting-cum-sampling opportunity to explore a region that is both beautiful and influential in the world of wine.

Talking points: The Loire is the longest river in France and, with its various tributaries, makes a huge range of wines, red, white, rosé, dry, sweet, semi-sparkling and sparkling. Kings and queens, poets, scholars, artists have all revelled in Loire wines. From Anjou, which everyone knows for its rosé, Henry Plantagenet, son of the local ruler, came to marry Eleanor, heiress of Aqcuitaine in 1152, and in 1154 they became King and Queen of England. The English crown owned a huge swathe of France, from the Loire to the Pyrenees. The regional gastronomy is, as might be expected, often based on fish (one famous recipe is for salmon poached in red wine) but there are also many pork and poultry recipes and superb fruits. There are many fairy-tale châteaux where the French court came to hunt in the open countryside and, although murders and poisonings took place in some of them, they generally housed queens, royal mistresses, noble ladies destined for great marriages and young men skilled in courtly accomplishments. The wines reflect this lightness and elegance of spirit, as you'll note if you visit the region.

TASTING NOTES

Chenin

The Chenin Blanc is a classic white wine grape and is grown all over the world. The wines it makes can be dry, medium dry, sweet sparkling. This example is young and very fresh, showing the overall style of a dry Chenin. You may care to try some of the South African Chenin wines, where sometimes the grape is given an Afrikaner name 'Steen' (see Session 9.) Most of the Loire sparkling wines are made from this grape.

Rémy Pannier, from whom this wine comes, is one of the great establishments at Saumur, where the pointed towers of the great castle soar above the river and the cadets of the famous cavalry school swagger the streets in their cloaks. The river banks, often actually below the vineyards, are hollowed with many caves and tunnels, formerly used for storage, today often in use by the wine trade for ideal maturation in the cool limestone cliffs.

The colour: Very pale, lightly shimmering lemon-yellow.

The smell: This too is light; shake the wine around in the glass to stress the smell. It suggests a dry wine, then, as the smell developes, it brings a fresh, very slightly intense smell that to me evokes the 'honey and flowers' impression you may remember from when you sucked the florets of clover as a child. This is typical Chenin, in whatever wine the grape features.

The flavour: Quite full – maybe you thought it was going to be somewhat thin, because of the initial impression of dryness? As you swallow, note that the 'honey and flowers' of gentle but fresh fragrance echoes around the mouth for quite a while – the wine has 'length'. It leaves a final impression of 'push' – it may begin delicately, but it is a firmish drink.

Sancerre 1983

You can see a picture of Sancerre on the label, a medieval walled town high above a curve of the Loire, dominating the vineyards. The goat on the label refers to the excellent local cheeses, small and round, known rather crudely, but in typical realistic French, as crottins or 'droppings'. They are good with both white and red wines. The grape used for Sancerre is the Sauvignon Blanc, a famous classic variety. Somehow, even in a blend, it always makes its presence felt in a wine. The 'cold steel' freshness often reminds me of the smell of an old steel knife as you wipe or sharpen it.

The colour: Also pale – but there's a bit more lemon tone. Don't forget that Sancerre is not far from Burgundy, but the wine from that region is made from a different grape and you'd note the difference in colour if you compared them side by side.

The smell: Another cool, crisply dry aroma. The Sauvignon invariably gets described as 'green' because of the delicious freshness when this grape makes wines in a fairly cool vineyard. If you can't find the 'cold steel', which sometimes seems more definite in the flavour, then see if the smell here evokes gooseberries. A Sauvignon from Bordeaux would smell slightly fuller; this one benefits from the more northerly situation.

The flavour: Quite full and fruity, the final impression being very crisp, toning up the palate – and making it want more! The after-taste, lingering on the palate, is verging on metallic, as if you'd been drinking out of a silver goblet.

Cabernet de Touraine 1983

This is the Cabernet Franc, one of the great grapes involved with claret or red Bordeaux, to which it gives zip and freshness. By itself it is much grown along the Loire, where its nickname is 'le Breton' after the man who brought it here from Bordeaux when the great Cardinal Richelieu was establishing vineyards around the planned town that bears his name. In a warm year it can show delicious fruitiness – alas, the British often find it 'sharp', which is exactly what it should be!

The colour: Dark purple-red, with a pinkish-lilac rim, where the wine meets the glass as you tilt it away from you and look at it over something white. This is a vigorous young wine and indeed this example should be drunk while young and charming.

The smell: The Cabernet Franc always says 'privet' to me – a leafy smell, like shrubberies after a shower. You don't get this sort of smell from a wine from a hot vineyard.

The flavour: Whether or not you serve it cool, notice the delicate fruitiness – this is a wine to drink in generous mouthfuls. It refreshes the palate just as a good eating apple does and you want to squeeze it around the gums and through the mouth. The slight 'lift' of extra crispness as the wine passes from the palate is attractive. This example came from a good year for this grape along the Loire – but the next vintage has been propitious as well, so that the wine is fully ripe.

Château du Breuil 1983, Coteaux du Layon

The Layon is a river that runs into the Loire, south of Angers. Here the Chenin Blanc produces a wide range of semi-sweet and sweet wines, all white, although there are a number of pink wines also made in the area. If you tour here, note the gently rolling countryside, the vineyards undulating above the river. The 'noble rot' special action on the grapes in a very ripe year makes the sweet wines definitely honeyed. You may hear the Chenin Blanc locally referred to as 'Pineau' or 'Pineau de la Loire' – this is its nickname, not to be confused with the great 'Pinot' family of grapes, both black and white, which are of a totally different strain.

The colour: Slightly more definite gold than for the dry Chenin and it will deepen more in tone with some age.

The smell: The 'honey and flowers' wafting fragrance is more apparent here, lightly alluring. You would not think this was going to be a dry wine – although in fact it is never cloyingly sweet and the wine could be happily enjoyed as a between-times refresher, if you were sitting out in the garden, enjoying some fresh fruit.

The flavour: The wine has a fine balance of fruit and acidity, which all good wine should have. So, although it's fairly full and ripe in taste, there's a 'grip' that prevents it from feeling sticky in the mouth. You will notice the honeyed character – it is quite firm – and this builds up to a definite and pleasant climax, so that, when you've drunk the wine, the final impression is quite strongly made. This really does register the Chenin Blanc when fully ripe!

Conclusion: Loire wines are still not well-known by British drinkers, apart from Muscadet and, maybe, Sancerre. But the variety is great and many qualities are made, so that they can be great value in different price ranges. Although many of them are elegant partners to fine food, they are uncomplicated and pleasant with many very casual dishes.

Alternatives: You could put Muscadet as an apéritif or first course wine with any Loire-orientated meal. There are also good Chenin Blanc dry wines from South Africa – the KWV Chenin is particularly agreeable (see Session 9). You could also start with the Sancerre, as most retailers will have this wine, even if not an exactly similar example. If the Cabernet Franc doesn't please you, then see if you can find a Gamay de Touraine. The Gamay grape is widely grown there and in fact it's said that, before controls became strict, plenty of the wine it made went down 'somewhere else' – that is, to the Beaujolais! Beaujolais is an easy choice if you want something else. There really isn't an alternative to the Château du Breuil, but the 'late picked' Chenin Blanc wines from the South African Cape, also made from the Chenin (or the Steen), are approximate possibilities.

Suggested food: A typical Loire-style meal might start with rillettes de porc (a rich pâté of pork), followed by salmon or salmon trout, hot or cold, then local cheeses – you could have the red wine with a goat cheese if not with the fish – and then fruit or a fruit tart or pastry with the sweet wine. More simply, you could make up a platter of fish, shellfish and crustacea, with mayonnaise, serve the red wine with cheese and a fruit fool with the sweet wine. Or, perhaps, start with a spinach or asparagus quiche, then roast chicken (possibly cooked with tarragon), hot or cold, and a cherry flan. The Sancerre is good, too, with taramasalata or white fish steaks, the Cabernet Franc with pork – even spareribs.

W   I   N   E   S

1 KWV Chenin Blanc 1982 (South Africa)
2 Houghton Supreme 1981 (Western Australia)
3 1982 Culemborg Pinotage (Paarl, South Africa)

Availability: Waitrose

Theme: Learning more about the Chenin Blanc with some southern hemisphere wines, and introducing an unusual grape – the Pinotage.

Practicalities: Chill the two white wines for an hour in the refrigerator or for fifteen minutes in a bucket of ice and water. Draw the cork on the Pinotage half an hour to an hour before you are going to drink it and, unless it's a warm day, stand the bottle in the room where the meal is to be served.

What you're aiming to do: Only fairly recently have wines from the southern hemisphere become widely available in the UK, but the impeccable standards of quality observed by the makers mean that most of them have great interest for European wine lovers. The Cape wines do display the character of wines from a hot vineyard, but the careful making ensures their freshness. The Australian wine shows a well-known grape plus a little addition of another – to make it especially interesting. The red wine, made from the Pinotage, combines the attributes of two classic wine grapes. The different foods and open air way of life in the Cape and many parts of Australia mean that white wine often serves as an apéritif or mid-day refresher, red wines being used for the gutsy foods often served at barbecues. Therefore, both sorts of wines have relevance to the UK now that 'cuisine' often sensibly gives way to traditional cooking.

Talking points: The first vines were planted at the Cape in 1652 and many of the estates making wine today have been doing so for over two centuries. Our ancestors prized the wines, even Napoleon in exile on St. Helena enjoyed them and their standards of cultivation and production are second to none in the world. The colour strips – the 'wine seal' – on the two bottles of this session indicate the grape ('cultivar' in the Cape), the vintage and the place of origin within one of the five main wine regions. Other strip seals indicate different details.

Australia is such a vast country that to generalise about its wines is like generalising about the wines of Europe! But Western Australia, homeland of this wine, is up and coming wine country; the south, where it's definitely cool and cold, making fine wine from many small estates, the middle region (this wine comes from the Middle Swan, the area around the Swan River that curves into Perth like a beautiful sickle) rich in quality wineries. Houghton make use of some of the most traditional vineyards and wineries and have some of the Western Australian wine dynasties contributing to their wines, yet their methods are completely advanced, combining old and new with tremendous success.

TASTING NOTES

KWV Chenin Blanc 1982

This is a wine from the Coastal region and is made by the KWV, the enormous co-operative that dominates the town of Paarl. It's thanks to the KWV that many Cape wine concerns have been able to continue making quality wines, although the concern doesn't sell its wine in the Cape at all. They perform great work in research, education and promotion and it is thanks to their courage at a depressed time years ago that the Cape wine industry has not only survived but has won the respect of even the most self-assured wine makers of the classic regions.

The colour: A pale but definite golden tone (if you get a younger vintage, this may be lighter, but this is a southern wine). The lemon tone will usually be slightly deeper than that of a European counterpart.

The smell: Here's the Chenin Blanc, much planted at the Cape, but doesn't it seem to have been grown in a warmer, sunnier vineyard than the Loire (Session 8)?

There's a full, slightly flowery smell, but not so much the piercing, honeyed aroma which you might detect in a Loire Chenin. It's direct, appealing, uncomplicated.

The flavour: Rather full and with undertones of an almost woody firmness – though this wine certainly hasn't ever been in cask! The 'bracken' note of the smell is more obvious in the taste – it's a very dry wine, yet with a firm, sharply defined style. Perhaps not with great length, but a nice mouthful to freshen the palate. The 1983 vintage is fuller, if you encounter this.

Houghton Supreme 1981

This wine is based on the Chenin Blanc, the wine grape that is so widely grown in the southern hemisphere. But it's had an addition of Muscadelle – giving it additional amiability, rather as a squeeze of lemon gives zip to many a sauce. Even competitors (and no one is more competitive than the Australian wine maker, because wine competitions make newspaper headlines in that country!) admit that this is a highly successful wine.

The colour: Golden-yellow, lightening a little at the rim where the wine meets the glass.

The smell: Certainly Chenin Blanc – but with a fatty aroma. The Sultan's harem has been enriched by a plump lady! That's the Muscadelle. Do you find a touch of spice, slightly exotic, in the aroma? It's not straight Chenin.

The flavour: Very full, very firm – surprisingly dry it may seem to many after the enticing smell. There's a touch of tropical fruit to my palate here – the warm, fat, mango-cum-papaya to those who've been lucky enough to taste them in their homeland. Note, though, the slightly 'chewy' substantial character, which makes the mouth-filling taste live up to the expectations of the smell and although the wine finishes dry, it's broad in the beam – only the skill of really good making prevents this being blowzy, but, as it is, this is a very attractive wine, maybe a little 'bosomy', certainly with interest along every stage of tasting. Later vintages have same overall style.

1982 Culemborg Pinotage

This is a wine from Paarl, the rocks above the Erste River gleaming like pearls hence the early settlers' name, Paarlis. It's also the longest main street in the Cape – I think seven miles, but it may be more! In former times, the holdings extended down to the river, but those would have been very long back gardens indeed. Today the charming Dutch houses (the beauty of the 'honeycomb' church in Paarl is breathtaking), the huge KWV establishment and, soaring above all, the 'Taal Monument' signifying the unity of the three languages of the Cape, make Paarl as impressive as it is important. The Pinotage is a grape variety evolved from the Pinot Noir, the great black grape of red Burgundy, and the Cinsaut or Cinsault, a grape that contributes to many Rhône wines (see Session 13). For some years I believed that Pinotage was only grown at the Cape – but Australia has begun to grow it! The variety possesses many attributes that are suited to consumer demands today.

The colour: Deep red – and, if you can think about it, a Burgundy and Rhône red rather than anything from the Bordeaux side of France (or a Cabernet Sauvignon grape). There's a little lightening at the rim of the wine.

The smell: A warm, inviting, sunny aroma – but totally different from the 'dusty road' smell of Rioja (see Session 12). This must be a wine from a warm, even hot vineyard, shoving itself forward, saying 'Enjoy me!'

The flavour: This is very full, slightly tough, certainly in the after-taste. The wine is a sultry, full-bodied example, with a delightful touch of fresh fruit in the final taste as it leaves the palate.

Conclusion: Anyone who supposes that Cape and Australian wines are 'poor relations' is in for a surprise – many authorities would price all these far higher as value for money in terms of quality. They are all wines made in clean, dry atmospheres – which must make some difference! Maybe none of these are in the 'complex' category – but, if you pay more for some of the estate wines of the various areas, you can get this too and the immediate pleasure is quite often far in advance of something bearing a fancy name and pretty label from some 'known name' in Europe.

Alternatives: There are plenty of good Cape wines in the UK and the Chenins are plentiful. Remember that an estate wine, for which you will pay more, will obviously have more to give in terms of subtlety. If you can keep to Western Australia, the wine may have some kinship to the example here, but they do grow plenty of Chenin – and even some Pinotage. There are some very fine estate Pinotage Cape wines on sale in the UK – it would flatter any wine lover to have the chance to compare them at an informal meal.

Suggested food: At the Cape, dry white wine is a general apéritif, so this KWV Chenin or, certainly, any similar wines would be entirely acceptable. The Pinotage is a gutsy wine, very much for barbecues, but where the fare includes the rich 'boerwurst' (farmers' sausages), plus steaks, kidneys and meats of every sort. You could offer, for a rather typical meal, slivers of smoked pork or beef, or simply cured ham as a starter, followed by either a mixed grill (fling everything into the pan) or black pudding, plus a selection of salads, and chunks of melon or fresh fruit. But, more easily, why not offer the Houghton wine with scampi in a rather garlicky sauce or simply fresh prawns, followed by a casserole of beef. Or, even easier, present diners with slices of asparagus quiche, the Houghton Supreme will be quite up to that, followed by the very best sausages you can find (or a selection) with mashed potatoes, to go with the Pinotage and with a pretty creamy fruit (or even chocolate) pudding to follow.

W	*I*	*N*	*E*	*S*

1 Apremont (Savoie) 1983
2 1983 Soave Classico, Masi
3 1983 Moulin-à-Vent, Pasquier Desvignes
4 1982 Brown Brothers Late Picked Muscat Blanc, Milawa
Estate (Victoria, Australia)

Availability: Oddbins

Theme: How an unknown wine can sharpen your perception and appreciation of the classics.

Practicalities: Chill the Apremont, the Soave and the Muscat Blanc, for an hour in the refrigerator or fifteen minutes in a deep bucket of ice and water. Leave all of them chilling until required, but draw the corks of the Soave and Muscat Blanc a few minutes in advance of drinking. The Moulin-à-Vent Beaujolais can be served at room temperature, but not too warm and you may even prefer to serve it slightly cool, as this is quite routine on a stuffy day in the wine's own region.

What you're aiming to do: A new and unusual wine can sharpen all the senses to a reappraisal and fresh appreciation of an old and familiar wine. Two of these wines may not be known as yet to even your wine-wise friends. Soave and Moulin-à-Vent are firm favourites already. This progression of wines is of a quality and interest that would be worthy of a meal aimed to please your most important guests, but each one will happily accompany last-minute improvisations or even the produce of the local delicatessen that stays open late. If you want to curtail the range, start with the Soave or Apremont (the latter is truly dry) or, if you need to, do without the late picked Muscat.

Talking points: Apremont is from Savoy, in the east of France, very beautiful countryside but tending to be known only to winter sports addicts. It's slightly fizzy – a frivolous comment might be that it's France's answer to Portugal's vinho verde! (see Session 5). Masi, whose firm make the Soave, are renowned wine makers from the Veneto region in north Italy (Session 7). Pasquier Desvignes are very old-established producers of Beaujolais and their 'house style' is particularly well-balanced, trim and elegant, always giving pleasure. Brown Brothers are one of the great wine families of Australia; the first John Brown settled at Milawa, in East Victoria, in 1889 and the firm is still a family concern, with the eldest son always being called John. They are respected wine makers, producing a huge range of wines from different single grape varieties.

TASTING NOTES

Apremont

This wine has been bottled 'sur lie', which means that it has gone straight into the bottle without being filtered or treated, thereby keeping the pronounced freshness and the mini-fizz that shows it is still lively, as it might be if remaining on its lees in cask or vat, with the wine yeasts endowing it with a pleasant little prickle of fizz. Muscadet is often bottled in this way. This Apremont comes from Montélimar – famous for nougat!

The colour: Very pale lemon – a coolish wine from a cool vineyard.

The smell: Fresh, almost saltily so. You expect a dry wine.

The flavour: There are the minute bubbles, indicating the 'sur lie' liveliness. Otherwise, the wine is straightforward, lightly fresh on the palate, developing a fullness in the middle taste.

Soave 1983

Soave is a delightful walled town, with the vineyards extending to the gates. Many styles of this popular wine are made, so don't expect all to be the same as this – which is a very fine one. Two grapes make it, but the one that you may register is only responsible for about 20%. This is a form of the Trebbiano grape, which, under other names, is also grown in France. To me the Trebbiano always wafts a vanilla and slightly herby smell to my nose and, in some Italian wines, it is so pronounced as to suggest toffee or caramels.

The colour: Pale, with a touch of straw.

The smell: Vanilla and a touch of spice, fresh, implying a cool character.

The flavour: Quite full in the mouth, with a touch of fat and firmness as it leaves the palate. Clean, trim, very well-made – note the crisp but fairly substantial 'finish'.

Moulin-à-Vent 1983

This particular 'cru' or growth of Beaujolais is one of the finest, possibly *the* finest. It is also one of the few growths that can benefit by some bottle-age, although no Beaujolais should be matured in bottle for as long as certain other fine red wines – its charm lies in its youth. A good Moulin-à-Vent is often described as having a 'steely' character. There *is* a windmill, a Moulin-à-Vent, in the village, which was formerly used for grinding the villagers' corn.

The colour: Impressively pleasing – a deep, brilliant red, with a touch of pink at the edges. Although young it is showing just a little shading of tones.

The smell: This is the Gamay grape really showing off! There is a whiff of fruit plus something a little more delicate and flowery – some people might detect a note of violets or spring flowers. Register this as true and typical Gamay in a good vintage, well made. The 1984 will be slightly fruitier and crisper.

The flavour: There is plenty of depth to this wine, although much Beaujolais is rather light in style – and agreeably so. Here there is an inner firm constitution, again, with a hint of steeliness if you can pick this up in the taste. It's crisp and vigorous, still obviously young, with an admirable flourish of flavour as it leaves the palate. A later vintage will be somewhat more assertive.

1982 Brown Brothers Late Picked Muscat Blanc, Milawa Estate

The Muscat is a large family of grapes, making wines dry, sweet and sometimes sparkling. But the one thing all have in common is that, unlike most wine grapes, the wine Muscats produce is obviously 'grapey' – but don't ever be misled by supposing that a Muscat wine, redolent with fruity charm, as you smell it, is then going to be very sweet – it may be bone dry! A Muscat d'Alsace, for example, will be a wine to drink as an apéritif or with certain dishes. This one, however, really is a sweet wine, though not quite what the Australians of its homeland would call a 'big sticky'.

The colour: A yellowish gold, which will darken as the wine ages more.

The smell: Definitely and obviously Muscat – it's like plunging your face into a bunch of very ripe white dessert grapes! The intense ripeness, resulting from the grapes being picked when they were fully ripe or, even, slightly over ripe, is balanced in this well-made example by an underlying freshness – again, just like the freshness of grapes.

The flavour: Quite a big wine, the taste coming on after the initial impression provided by the smell. Note the way in which, although the wine is sweet, verging on luscious, there is a good balance between the rich fruit and the acidity, which keeps the wine in proportion. A wine that is *just* richly sweet is not easy to go on drinking – if you think of a comparison between chocolate cream cake and a bunch of Muscat grapes, you'll understand that it's easier to continue eating the fruit when the cake begins to cloy the palate and cut the appetite. The taste lingers in the mouth even after you've swallowed the wine – there is considerable 'length' here. Register the intense overripeness of the grapes that have made this wine – the vineyard is a hotter one than the vineyards of the Coteaux du Layon (see Session 8) or those around Bordeaux (see Session 4), but you can admire the skill with which this sweet wine remains well-proportioned, whereas very hot regions tend to make wines that are solely and merely sweet, somewhat lacking in fragrance or complexity.

Conclusion: Among the well-known favourite wines of Europe, such as Soave and Beaujolais (Moulin-à-Vent), it's important to differentiate between producers who make typical wines of a high standard of quality. Because of the popularity of these wines, some rather insipid or even dreary examples can be made – of course, you pay for quality, but, seeing wines such as those mentioned here, it's worth it for the little extra, rather than the cheap but dubious 'bargain' from some unknown source. The 'new' wines are in the 'have to try harder' category and always provide interest even for the experienced drinker. From the New World, great value and fascination is available, from individual producers and vineyards. Remember, it's as silly to generalise about 'Australian wines' as it would be to generalise about 'European wines' – Australia is such a vast continent that tremendous variety is available, even within the same region.

Alternatives: There really isn't one for the Apremont, but you could substitute a vinho verde. Many firms make Soave – but don't be lured into buying too cheap a bottle and the same applies to all Beaujolais, especially Moulin-à-Vent, which is never in the lower price ranges. Or you could try a straight Gamay. There are no obvious alternatives to the late picked Muscat Blanc, but you might try one of the late picked South African wines, although these will be from different grapes or a Coteaux du Layon (Session 8) or maybe a Loupiac (Session 4).

Suggested food: Both the Apremont and the Soave could be apéritif drinks, or go with many first courses. The Beaujolais is probably best with meat, roasts and grills, and the Muscat Blanc with some version of a fruity pudding. You could have trout with toasted almonds as the first course, followed by roast veal (in the region they might have roast rabbit or rabbit with a mustard sauce – mild mustard), plus cheese and then the Australian Pavlova would go with the sweet wine. But an easier meal could be a pâté of fish or smoked fish, perhaps with a green sauce, then pigeon or chicken in a casserole and apple charlotte or a salad of kiwi fruit, plus some of the sweet wine. If you are cutting one of the wines out, then serve one of the whites as the apéritif, have a vegetable soup with no wine, then chicken and ham pie or veal and ham pie and grapes to go with the Muscat Blanc.

1 Grenache rosé, vin de table
2 Vin de pays de l'Uzège.

Availability: Victoria Wine

Theme: Registering hot vineyard southern black grapes with wines from the vineyards in the south of France.

Practicalities: Chill the rosé wine for a quarter of an hour in a deep bucket of ice and water, or put it in the refrigerator for an hour. Chill the light red wine too, but for slightly less time.

What you're aiming to do: Many people suppose that wines of the holiday regions, such as Provence, are 'light' in style, because they may look light in colour. In fact many of these wines are quite robust enough to be served with the sort of informal, semi-picnic, almost buffet food that can be taxing to anything delicate. The two examples here are ideal for casual, peasant fare which can be so welcome a reminder of 'the sun and old stones' even on a chilly wet day.

Talking points: The Grenache grape is very widely grown in many vineyards (in Spain it's the Garnacha). It makes a wide variety of wines in the Rhône Valley. The little Uzège wine is a real novelty – from the region around Uzès in Provence. In addition to the Grenache, it's made from the Syrah, the black grape that gives perfume and nobility to many Rhône wines, also the Cinsault, another widely-grown variety here, and the Mourvèdre, another grape originating in Spain and, today, becoming known for its contribution to the wines of Bandol and the Côtes de Provence (and Rhône, see Session 16).

Grenache Rosé

The rosé wines of this part of the world are famous – you may have already tried Tavel. But the Grenache grape gives them some assertiveness and fullness and this one shows off the style of the sort of wine that's very evocative of holiday countryside, warm and slightly soft.

The colour: Clear, salmony pink, definitely from a warm vineyard.

The smell: Quite full and fruity – the Grenache often gives me the slight whiff of a dusty highway under the sun, very 'baked'. The next time you sample a Rioja or Penedés red wine or another Rhône red, see if you pick up a similar smell.

The flavour: Quite a lot of fruit here as well, in balance with the smell. There's a touch of what is almost oiliness as the wine runs over the palate. If you tasted this blindfold, you might well take it for a light-bodied red.

Vin de Pays de l'Uzège

Uzès is an old and historic walled town but, for the wine minded, it's interesting because it is placed on a plateau of chalky, limestone soil, admirable for many vines and conducive to the making of wines that possess a delicacy and neat charm, even when they are made on a fairly modest scale. This is a very good example of a pretty little modern wine.

The colour: Light red, with a touch of cherry tone.

The smell: A touch of something warm here, with a rather full, verging on soft aroma. Some of the wines from these remind me of the 'garrigue', the great, pastures that are redolent of herbs and tiny flowers so that, when the wind blows, there are numerous spicy, slightly scented smells to note.

The flavour: Again, a wine that's obviously been sunbaked, but has been well made so that it's trim and in balance. The touch of softness comes from the Mourvèdre, the slightly firm flavour from the Syrah, plus the fruitiness of the Grenache and a little hardness from the Cinsault, to hold everything together, the final flavour being quite definite.

Conclusion: Grapes that make the wines of the 'warm south' can, thanks to modern methods of wine making, produce wines that are attractive as well as impressive – but they do possess a slightly robust, peasant quality that makes them far more assertive than mere 'holiday drinks'.

Alternatives: The Grenache rosé really has no substitute, but there are plenty of Rhône rosé wines – try those of Lirac, Cairanne and many others. The Uzège is another novelty, but if you can't find either of these wines, try inexpensive Rhône or Provence wines – those of the Côtes de Provence and Bandol and Tavel will, however, be more expensive.

Suggested food: These two wines are excellent to partner a buffet and very useful anyway for accompanying southern-style dishes – whether or not you're a lover of garlic! Olives, radishes, slivers of raw carrot and florets of cauliflower with a 'dip' of cream cheese made piquant with paprika, or aioli, the provençal garlic mayonnaise, plus coarse pâté, anchovies, stuffed peppers, ratatouille, colourful salads of both fish and meat, tomatoes cooked with courgettes, stuffed aubergines, rice salads with mushrooms and sweetcorn, chunks of several sorts of melon, fresh peaches and apricots, nougat (the nougat capital of the world is Montélimar), or ices will all be delights. As the great Elizabeth David has remarked, even the simplest fare in this attractive part of France can have the appearance of a still-life: spread gingham cloths (or paper ones), provide some goat cheeses and use bright coloured plates for a meal with built-in sunshine. Even if you're restricted to more modest food, you can select a few items from a delicatessen to evoke the south, such as slices of garlic sausage; make a salad of tuna fish, sardines, or any rice, peppers, mushrooms, tomatoes and onion concoction. There are many suitable recipes or, simplest of all, you can serve these wines with scrambled eggs and home-made tomato sauce, made while you nibble the olives that are inseparable from the region's dishes.

W   I   N   E   S

1 Vouvray 1983
2 Morio Muskat (Rheinpfalz)
3 1975 Marqués de Romeral Rioja (optional)

Availability: Marks & Spencer

Theme: Introducing the Morio Muskat grape, trying a variation on the Loire Chenin Blanc and learning to recognise the distinctive Rioja.

Practicalities: Chill the two white wines for an hour in a refrigerator or fifteen minutes in a deep bucket of ice and water. Draw the corks five or ten minutes before you are going to drink them. Put the Rioja in the room where you are going to drink it and, if possible, draw the cork an hour ahead of drinking time.

What you're aiming to do: As you probably know, the 'white with white meat and fish, red with red meat and game' precept certainly isn't observed by the lucky people who live in wine regions! They drink whichever sort of wine they feel like drinking – or what's available. It's true, however, that some people find that, if they drink red wine while they're eating fish, they get a metallic taste in their mouths and many white wines are swamped by meat dishes, so that the drinker merely gets an impression of wine, rather than being able to enjoy the detailed flavour of the wine. The two white wines of this session are very different and would make an interesting comparison if you served them side by side at a meal. The red wine is not only an admirable example of Rioja, but is the sort of accompaniment that will stand up to many dishes that really are difficult to fit to many wines, including the sort of fish and meat mixtures that are found in many regional recipes of Europe.

Talking points: Vouvray is on the north bank of the River Loire and, although the vineyards spread far around it, there are some that are actually on top of the outcrops of limestone that forms the cellars where much of the wine is matured. The Morio Muskat is an example of a fairly recently evolved type of grape, already very popular. Rioja is certainly Spain's best-known table wine; it had a system of quality controls centuries ago and, as one of the men of Columbus' crew was a man from Rioja, it's possible that it was the first wine from Europe to reach the New World.

If you want to drink the white wines with the main courses of the meal, you can always serve the red one at the end, with cheese.

TASTING NOTES

Vouvray 1983

Here's the Chenin Blanc, one of the major white grapes of the Loire, but making a wine rather different in character from the Chenin of Session 8. Vouvray makes wine from very dry to extremely sweet and luscious, also wines that are pétillant (slightly sparkling) and fully sparkling.

The colour: Light, lemony gold tone.

The smell: Immediately evocative of warmth and ripeness – in fact this vintage was a warm one, so, if you have another vintage, there may be a hint of coolness. There's the honeyed, flowery fragrance typical of the Chenin Blanc.

The flavour: A very full, firm wine – people who categorise Vouvray as always being 'light' are generalising unwisely, because it can be graceful but definite. The way it leaves the palate is, after a middle taste of slight sweetness, crisp and refreshing.

Morio Muskat

This wine gets its name from Peter Morio, who ran the Viticultural Research establishment in Bavaria and first cultivated this strain. This sample comes from the Rheinpfalz or Palatinate region, very picturesque, where the wines usually possess an appealing style and, unlike some of the German wines, are good with many sorts of food.

The colour: Very pale – is there just a touch of light straw yellow tone?

The smell: Definitely Muskat (Muscat)! The grapiness is pronounced, but there is also a note of a fat, full 'something' that leads on to the taste.

The flavour: Quite full-bodied and with the touch of spiciness that is often found in Palatinate wines. This wine definitely gives the impression of sweetness in an uncomplicated way, but it is certainly not too sweet to accompany many foods.

1975 Marqués de Romeral Rioja

Rioja wines in former times were often kept for many years in cask – there are streets in the main wine villages where carts were not allowed to rumble over the cellars where the precious stuff was stored below ground! This is why some Riojas are still traditionally 'oaky', how much rather depends on the bodega (winery) or the individual maker. A mixture of grapes is generally used, according to the precise area and the water.

The colour: Mid-flame in tone, with a lightening at the edge where the wine meets the glass. Some Riojas can be very dark, but this one is gracefully shaded. If you are trying an example of a later vintage, it may be a little deeper-toned.

The smell: This is very definitely Rioja – with the oakiness that is so much liked coming through the warmth of the aroma. Although the region can be very cold in winter, this is definitely a 'warm vineyard' smell.

The flavour: Very well balanced as regards both the acidity and tannin – although the tannin is now less obvious, as the wine has some age to it. Although a firm wine, it's also trim and not aggressive – sometimes you require a 'pushy' big Rioja, but this is not in that genre. Everything about it is typical of its region, but it is not so 'regional' as to be difficult for anyone to like – sometimes wines of a very definite character can be offputting at the outset. This is a very nice example of Rioja indeed and one to register the wine in general. Does this wine remind you at all of those made from the Grenache in other areas – because there is likely to be some Garnacha in it?

Conclusion: The mixing of wines is one of the fascinations of wine drinking and people can argue the 'what with what' points for ever. It's fine to serve a regional wine with a regional recipe, but it's not always easy to work out and the range of wines you can introduce to friends can make a great deal of memorable difference even to a simple meal.

Alternatives: Vouvray (but remember it should be medium dry), Morio Muskat and Rioja are all now fairly generally available, although remember that although the Morio Muskat may not be very different in character if you have to get it from some other outlet there may be a great deal of difference between this Vouvray and Rioja and others – and a considerable price difference.

Suggested food: You could serve fish or rather plainly cooked poultry – maybe a chicken casserole with some of the wine in it, or cold chicken with a creamy sauce, also with wine in it. The Vouvray will go with fish such as hake, whiting, plaice or steaks of the big fat fish, turbot and halibut and, of course, salmon. Don't make any sauce too piquant, but it can be rich with butter and cream – and wine. The Morio Muskat could be good with cold fish, or, as might be served in the Palatinate, with cold cuts, such as sausages, salami, loin of pork. The Rioja might well accompany a paella in its homeland, or a pork or even game casserole. For an 'important' meal, using all the wines, you could start with a mousse or pâté of fish, following with baked gammon (hot or cold) and offer the Morio Muskat with the sweet course, such as a shortcake of fruit or lemon filled with fresh fruit – and some of the wine spooned on beforehand. You could use the Vouvray as an apéritif, or, if you're going straight to the red wine, the Morio Muskat, or vinho verde (Session 5).

| *W* | *I* | *N* | *E* |

Syrah de l'Ardèche

Availability: Cullens

Theme: Registering the Syrah grape.

Practicalities: This wine can be served at room temperature, but is also pleasant very slightly cool on a stuffy day. Anyway, draw the cork half an hour before you serve it. You can, as will be indicated, put it into a Rhône Valley session or serve it on its own as a fairly 'new' wine of agreeable character and versatility.

What you're aiming to do: The Syrah or, as it's sometimes called, the Shiraz, is a very old grape variety. It's not often used entirely by itself for wine in Europe, but yields most satisfactorily in many New World countries – though don't be misled into thinking that the 'Petite Sirah' of California is the same grape, because this is now believed to be a variety called the Durif. The Syrah contributes special quality to many of the Rhône Valley wines, providing the 'bloom' of the bouquet and the elegance to many.

Talking points: The Ardèche is a region that will be unknown to many. It's west of the Rhône and makes red, white and pink wines. Thanks to increased knowledge of vines and wine making and the ability to draw on the resources of advanced knowledge, some very pretty little wines come from such regions today.

The colour: A plum-pinky red.

The smell: Register the insinuating and charming aroma of fruit that the Syrah puts out – this is only a small-scale wine, but you may encounter this smell in the more important southern hemisphere Syrah/Shiraz wines.

The flavour: Very easy drinking, light-bodied, but quite full in the mouth. There are times when you want to get one single impression from a wine and this provides it – the Syrah in miniature. After that, all you have to do is drink and enjoy!

Alternatives: There are Cape and Australian Shiraz wines, but these may well be vintage wines and of greater character, perhaps very slightly 'jammy' which is something you may pick up in the after-taste of this Syrah, which to me is very lightly evocative of squashed raspberries. Otherwise, you may try a Côtes du Rhône from the north of the region, from a good shipper, which will usually have a high proportion of Syrah in it, or, in finer wines, be 100 per cent Syrah.

Suggested food: If you wish, put this wine into any of the sessions where Rhône Valley wines are being appraised; use it as the preliminary 'mouth wash'. Otherwise, it can partner the Cinsault/Syrah (Session 14) for informal meals, even sandwiches, or a pasta or rice dish.

W	*I*	*N*	*E*

Cante Cigale, Cinsault/Syrah

Availability: Waitrose

Theme: The Syrah plus the Cinsault – an example of how modern wine-making techniques make good small-scale classics.

Practicalities: Don't serve this wine too 'chambré' or tepid. Indeed, if you propose to drink it in stuffy weather, you can polish it up considerably if you put the bottle in the refrigerator for half an hour or plunge it into a bucket of ice and water for 5–10 minutes.

What you're aiming to do: The Syrah/Sirah/Shiraz/Schiras is one of the oldest known wine grapes in the world. It may have come from Persia. Today it's found mainly in the Rhône Valley, although there are plantations of it in some New World vineyards, where it can make very fine wines. It is a grape that can convey nobility, so it's worth registering. The Cinsault/Cinsault is used much in various blends of wines, giving a softness and added fragrance when it's made in conjunction with the Grenache and Carignan. In this wine you are registering the contributions of these two grapes – and enjoying the result.

Talking points: This is a good example of a small-scale red wine that will vary slightly from vintage to vintage – vintages do vary here, but the wine won't get better if 'laid down', so you should drink it while it's young. There's a mistaken idea that old wine is invariably better wine, but that only applies to the very finest wines in certain vintages. This wine is made to be enjoyable soon after it's bottled – if you kept it, it would become 'tired' and lose its delightful fruitiness in two or three years. Although wines from the Syrah can have moderately long lives, the Cinsault doesn't contribute longevity.

TASTING NOTES

The colour: Purplish-red, with a lilac-toned rim where the wine meets the glass.

The smell: The slightly herby, aromatic waft is indicative of the presence of the Syrah. Note this, so that you pick it out when trying more important Rhône wines (see Session 16). The smell is immediate, obvious.

The flavour: There's an agreeable roundness, with a firm inner flavour, that, until you aerate the wine a little, is almost tough. This is part of the contribution of the Cinsault – the taste could pass quickly from the palate, but this firmness keeps it on, the fruit and herby indications provided by the smell being maintained.

Conclusion: This delicious 'little' wine contributes some experience of two important red wine grapes, notably, by its smell, the Syrah.

Alternatives: There isn't an equivalent of the Cante Cigale (Singing Cricket) wine – although it's often available in a white version too. What you could do is to find a somewhat more expensive Côtes du Rhône, from a respected shipper, such as Paul Jaboulet, that will demonstrate in a very impressive way the characteristics of a predominantly Syrah-based wine. As there are many grapes – white as well as red – permitted in Rhône reds, it's risky to generalise too much, but, in the north of the region, it tends to be the Syrah that yields the quality wines, the Grenache (see Session 11) being used in some of the Châteauneuf du Pape and more southern Rhône wines to a more obvious extent.

Suggested food: This is virtually a when-in-doubt red wine for any time. But you could put it into a more formal progression of wines to introduce an important red Rhône – remember, any fine wine always tastes better if prefaced by something more modest, and the first wine tends to seem better too. Serve it with a bread and cheese meal, or a fairly lightly-flavoured pasta dish, such as lasagne, or a potato gratin that includes cheese and perhaps anchovies and tomatoes (the wine is robust enough) or a chicken liver risotto or that favourite nursery dish, macaroni cheese. You could preface it with a vinho verde (Waitrose have a good one) or any dryish white wine or vermouth and simply offer it with an assortment of cold meats, or good sandwiches (wholemeal bread for some) of various meats, cheeses and with a light salad.

```
┌─────────────────────────────┐
│   TASTING    SESSION        │
│  ┌───────────────────────┐  │
│  │                       │  │
│  │         15            │  │
│  │                       │  │
│  └───────────────────────┘  │
└─────────────────────────────┘
```

W	I	N	E	S

1 Vin de pays, Côtes de Gascogne blanc
2 Foncalieu Cabernet Sauvignon 1982, vins de pays de l'Aude
3 Montana Marlborough Province Cabernet Sauvignon 1979, product of New Zealand

Availability: Waitrose

Theme: Finding out more about the Cabernet Sauvignon grape.

Practicalities: Chill the white wine for a quarter of an hour in a deep bucket of ice and water or for an hour in the refrigerator. Draw the cork of the Foncalieu half an hour to an hour beforehand, draw the cork of the Marlborough Cabernet an hour to an hour and a half beforehand.

What you're aiming to do: The Cabernet Sauvignon is one of the great classic wine grapes of the world – some people would say it's *the* supreme black grape. It's grown in many vineyards and of course it varies according to the region, the maker and the style of the winery. Because it attracts so much attention, it's interesting to register. Sometimes people find it difficult to like because, used as a single grape variety in a wine, it can seem stiff, harsh and what I often think of as 'bony'. Here, however, two wines show how agreeable as well as impressive it can be. The little white wine from a little-known grape is the sort of wine that wouldn't have been made fresh, crisp and lightly dry until very recently – it's these small-scale local wines that give us all so much pleasure, thanks to modern techniques of wine making. (see Session 4.)

Talking points: The Côtes de Gascogne wine will be a novelty to many, although anyone lucky enough to go down to the beautiful region in the south-west of France may have enjoyed it on the spot. It's also made from grapes that are unlikely to be widely known. The two red wines are specially interesting examples: the wine from the Aude because of the way it's made, the 'kiwi wine' because of where it comes from. But the two are excellent examples of what is possibly the most famous black grape in the world of wine.

TASTING NOTES

Côtes de Gascogne

The Columbard grape from which this is chiefly made is known in the Cognac region, where it contributes to the white wine that's distilled there. But it's also grown in other countries now and makes an agreeable lightweight drink.

The colour: Pale straw-gilt, fairly light but definite in tone.

The smell: A waft of warmth seems to come up from the glass – it's from a sunny vineyard and is straightforwardly pleasant.

The flavour: Surprisingly full in the mouth and agreeably fruity – has been described as a 'fruit salad' type of wine! Notice the crisp, zippy finish. Nothing complicated about this wine, but it's first-rate 'mouth wash' before something more important.

Foncalieu Cabernet Sauvignon 1982, vin de pays de l'Aude

The vins de pays are the regional wines that are subject to controls, like those of appellation contrôlée, and they represent excellent value these days, showing their regional style and, often, having great individuality. The Aude is a southern region, where, formerly, vast amounts of wine were made that were rather 'ordinary' and were sold to the vermouth makers. Now these 'little wines' are coming into their own. This example is interesting, because in France the Cabernet Sauvignon grape is best known for its presence in the red wines of Bordeaux, but with other grapes as well (See Session 4). Here it's used on its own but, because it might have a touch of hardness that would unbalance it, there's a proportion of wine made according to what's called the 'macération carbonique' method. No need to worry too much about this, but it's the means whereby what could have been hard, stiff, tough and purely 'local' wines can be given a softer, more fluid character, while retaining their regional style, and that enables them to be ready to enjoy while quite young. This wine wouldn't improve if you put it away for years – but it's delicious to drink now.

The colour: A bright, clear red-pink, with a touch of blue tone at the edge where it meets the glass.

The smell: Light but assertive and very fresh. To me, the Cabernet Sauvignon always has a slightly 'leafy' smell, of fresh vegetation. Here it is very true to itself – try to register the fragrance.

The flavour: Quite mouth-filling, note how it seems to spread out over the palate. There's additional freshness, the follow-up of the smell, plus quite a substantial taste – some Cabernet Sauvignon wines are occasionally described as 'chewy' and although this is a small-scale one, you can see that it's quite full. As it leaves the palate there's a delightful after-taste or back-taste ('huff' air down your nose and out of your mouth to note this), the grape registers itself typically.

Montana Marlborough Cabernet Sauvignon 1979

New Zealand has been making wines since the beginning of the nineteenth century and, in late Victorian times, they won international awards in Europe. They are not at all like most Australian wines – New Zealand is a cooler, more temperate country and one is never far from water. The wineries today have benefited enormously from sending their young wine makers to study abroad, notably in the US, and both family firms and big establishments are producing wines of all types that are already very pleasant and may well be impressive and great in only a short time. Marlborough Province is at the tip of the South Island, whereas most of the wineries are in the North Island, not far from Auckland, so the climate of Marlborough will be even cooler.

The colour: Far more shading of tones in this example – well, it's a more important and complex wine. The sample I tasted was showing a slightly tawny rim, but if you get a younger vintage (vintages don't vary very much here), it may not show this lightening as yet.

The smell: Very definitely fresh leaves! There's an attractive clean smell overall and then the 'shrubbery after a shower' freshness as I often describe it.

The flavour: Quite 'important' and full-bodied, with considerable length – this is the way in which the flavour lingers on the palate even after you've swallowed or spat out the wine. There are several flavours to think about, with the structure of the wine well-defined. Note the touch of tannin – the Cabernet Sauvignon usually makes a fairly tannic wine, which is why the great Cabernets can have such long lives – plus the zip and crispness of the fruit acidity. If you compared this Cabernet wine with one from a hotter vineyard, such as parts of California or Australia or the Cape, you would, I think, register its freshness, which prevents it being too assertively 'Cabernet', as I sometimes comment with warmer vineyard versions.

Conclusion: The Cabernet Sauvignon doesn't get its worldwide reputation for nothing! But, in making imposing and often wonderfully detailed and long-lived wines, care must be taken that these remain in proportion – you don't want a wine to kick you in the palate, after all. The interest and charm of fine Cabernet should touch the intelligence as well as being enjoyable.

Alternatives: There isn't anything to substitute for the white wine, although there are usually plenty of pleasant vins de pays around these days. You could simply offer a toning up apéritif of chilled Chambéry vermouth (Waitrose do a good one under their own label) and add a dash of soda if you want to keep yourself and your palate in reserve for maximum attention to the Cabernets.

Suggested food: Virtually any grilled or roast meat will be fine, although claret lovers often prefer lamb to beef when trying red Bordeaux. For a rather special menu you might have mushrooms au gratin as a starter and indulge yourselves with a millefeuilles or similar creamy, jam-enriched pastry afterwards. However, it's worth having even a little cheese to finish the two red wines, because this will not only make them taste even better, it will possibly show how various aspects of their taste develop during the meal. An easier meal might be pipérade to start with, then kebabs of lamb, followed by a fruit mousse, although you could serve the white wine as an apéritif and either omit any first course or else have a vegetable soup (vichyssoise or gazpacho) followed by a casserole of lamb and cheese and fruit.

W	I	N	E	S

1 Dry vermouth as apéritif
2 Beaujolais Blanc (Louis Jadot)
3 Gigondas 1982
4 Muscat de Beaumes de Venise, Domaine de Durban

Availability: Victoria Wine

Theme: Introducing the Chardonnay grape, trying the Muscat grape in its sweet form and getting to know a good Rhône wine.

Practicalities: Chill the Beaujolais Blanc for about an hour (not longer) in the refrigerator or ten minutes in a bucket of ice and water. Chill the Muscat de Beaumes de Venise at the same time and leave it in refrigerator or ice bucket until five or ten minutes before you wish to serve it, then draw the cork and replace this lightly. Put the glasses for this in the refrigerator if you've got the space, so that they will be cold when you pour the wine – this will make them pleasantly pearly to look at.

What you're aiming to do: You're entertaining someone of fair importance – whether an in-law, the boss or an influential friend. You know they are quite interested in wine and you may have been tempted to 'play safe' by choosing, for example, a white Burgundy or a dry German wine with the first course, a claret or, perhaps, a Burgundy with the main course and you wonder about something sweet to conclude. But *don't* play safe – if the guests know about wine, they'll be far more interested in trying something they may not drink often at home. This progression of wines works up to a high ending note and, whether or not you can stretch the budget to a fine roast, the red wine will please.

Talking points: White Beaujolais is something that has only been evolved in recent years. Beaujolais, says the conservative, must be *red* (see Tasting Session 10). But it's made from the Chardonnay grape, one of the great classic white grapes of the world and has become very chic, notably in the US. Gigondas is also a fairly 'new' name on lists although it's been making good red wine for centuries – in the past lots of it was sold as Châteauneuf du Pape. Our ancestors loved this type of wine and, with roasts and game, it really is an appropriate choice, far more satisfying to the person who knows wine other than a red Burgundy from no-one knows whom, that may be a sticky and dreary tipple. The sweet wine is a beauty – it charms novice and connoisseur alike and simplifies as well as delighting the end of the meal.

TASTING NOTES

Beaujolais Blanc

Try to get a fairly recent vintage of this wine. It comes from the respected establishment of Louis Jadot and is made entirely from the Chardonnay. You could offer it as an apéritif if people like a truly dry wine.

The colour: Light, very pale golden.

The smell: It is quite assertive – the Chardonnay can have a piercing bouquet. Indeed, if you serve a slightly softer wine before a Chardonnay, the Chardonnay will cut through it quite ruthlessly and you'll probably not be wholly pleased with either wine.

The flavour: Full, mouth-filling, a certain amount of charm, although this is always a rather austere wine and it finishes definitely dry. It makes itself known to the drinker, whether it's liked or not!

Gigondas 1982

Gigondas got its appellation contrôlée as recently as 1971. The Grenache is the predominant grape (see Tasting Session 11) but others in the blend may be the Syrah, Cinsault, Mourvèdre and Clairette. The Grenache may not contribute more than 65% to the wine, but it's very much in evidence in this sample. Our ancestors loved the Rhône wines and one famous writer described one of them as 'the manliest I ever drank'. They are particularly good with many traditional British recipes.

The colour: Definite red, fairly dark.

The smell: The 'dusty road' smell that I often note with certain wines where the Grenache plays a part is evident here, with an assertive, firm indication of the flavour.

The flavour: A firm wine, still inclined to be close in texture; what I mean by this is that it doesn't immediately open up to reveal what it does taste like, but is reserved. It's quite a cosy drink, comfortable and four-square, with a warm taste and a slightly crisp finish.

Muscat de Beaumes de Venise, Domaine Durban

This, say respected authorities, of the Beaumes de Venise Muscats, is the finest wine in the category of 'vin doux naturel' in the south of France. It can't be cheap, because it's slightly above table wine strength, so that extra duty is exacted. Beaumes was a Roman spa and the wines of the region have been enjoyed by successive Popes and hymned by poets. Red wine is made here, but it's the white Muscats that are famous; this is the only place in the Côtes du Rhône where Muscat vines are planted. This variety of Muscat, not to be confused with the Muscadelle grape, is one called Muscat à petits grains, though there are many in the Muscat family. The grape was known in Rome and even ancient Greece. It is planted in many countries, making dry as well as sweet wines – and sparkling wines. It's the one wine grape that makes wines that immediately evoke grapes ·as you smell them – therefore, in any blind tasting, it can be helpful to pick out a Muscat as a 'marker' wine. It is not always given a vintage date and, in its homeland, is drunk with much pleasure as an apéritif, but if you wish to try this, then I suggest putting it alongside a melon first course (as in the region) because any dry wine will seem hard and acid after it. (You can keep it, cool, for two to three weeks after opening.)

The colour: Bright, definite gleaming gold – this is nothing to do with the wine's age, because it's non-vintage, it's just typical of the Muscat here.

The smell: Definitely the Muscat grape! You plunge your nose into it, as into a bunch of grapes. But note the fresh, lightly fruity smell that also comes through – this isn't just a sweet wine, it's a fine one with lots of characteristics to appreciate.

The flavour: Full, but finely-balanced. This wine is firm, even assertive, but the see-saw of the fruit and acidity is still there – it isn't merely fat and sweet. (Rather like one of the delectable beauties of the region, it has an assurance – it knows how attractive it is, but doesn't waggle its hips in a vulgar way, it merely smiles.) Note how fresh the palate is left after you've swallowed the wine – there's a fascinating cool 'push' at this stage that makes this kind of wine very 'moreish'.

Conclusion: These wines would interest and impress the most knowledgeable. You have been able to study the Chardonnay grape, take another view of the Muscat in its sweet form, and get to know a Rhône wine that is still not expensive and most enjoyable with quite important but fairly gutsy food.

Alternatives: Beaujolais Blanc is sometimes listed among the UK retailers, otherwise look for a straight Chardonnay grape – although it won't have the touch of the sun prevalent here. The Gigondas may be found fairly widely – if you really cannot discover one, try a Châteauneuf du Pape, although this wine comes from a big area and, according to makers, can vary widely in style. The Muscat de Beaumes de Venise is becoming popular (each wine establishment will have its own version). All will be individual but have something in common.

Suggested foods: If you're able to eke out the housekeeping, try, for a really important meal, a starter of oeufs en gelée, or shrimps in a cream sauce, followed by roast beef (with all the British trimmings) or, more easily, a casserole of game (even pigeon, with olives), or steak and kidney pudding or pie, plus then some cheese, followed by any meringue-cum-spun-sugar-cum-fruit sweet dish you can rely on cooking well – or creme brûlée, for the Muscat will stand up even to this eggy dish. More economically, start with hardboiled eggs and tomatoes with mayonnaise, followed by baked ham or gammon – hot or cold – with a potato purée or lightly seasoned potato salad and a portion of cheese with melon afterwards.

If you wish, try the Muscat wine with a first course of melon and raw ham, after an apéritif of the Beaujolais Blanc, but keep enough back to serve a little more Muscat with the sweet – an ice or sorbet.

W   I   N   E   S

1 Bellingham Cape Gold
2 Cuvée Latour 1982, Louis Latour
3 Côtes de Beaune Villages 1982, Delamont
4 Hautes Côtes de Nuits Villages 1979, Joseph Drouhin.

Availability: Threshers; Ashe & Nephew

Theme: Burgundy – more about the Chardonnay and learning how to recognise the Pinot Noir.

Practicalities: Chill the Bellingham and the Cuvée Latour for an hour in the refrigerator or fifteen minutes in a deep bucket of ice and water; when you take out the Bellingham, you can leave the Cuvée Latour in the cool until you're ready for it. Draw the corks of the two red Burgundies half an hour in advance of trying the wines.

What you're aiming to do: Burgundy is a much-abused name in wine. The area is smaller than that of Bordeaux and, because it's so popular, high prices have to be paid for the finer wines – no use condemning the way they soar, if people are prepared to pay double figures, it's silly to blame the supplier who can get the price. What is silly, though, is to try to find a really cheap Burgundy – you may get one, from an unknown source, that is second or third rate as a wine anyway and does not represent this great region. Nowadays, some areas are being taken into the Burgundy vineyard, often with rather modest names, but, from reputable sources, offering value and quality. Famous establishments, too, are making up and selling wines they themselves drink frequently, that may bear humble A.O.C.s, but can be far better wines than something with a fancy label and only the faintest resemblance to 'the real thing' when you taste it.

Talking points: It's relevant to refer you to the comments about claret and red Burgundy (Session 4). But it's also pertinent to comment on those ambitious menus that feature both claret and Burgundy. In theory there is no obvious reason why this shouldn't be successful, although most books will recommend that you serve the claret before the red Burgundy. I suppose that, if an elaborate formal menu, such as was featured in former times is planned, then, with a sorbet to clear the palate between the first part of the meal, which may consist of various dishes culminating in a roast, it is possible to serve a red Burgundy with the game dish that comes later. But although I've eaten such meals, I can't say that they have impressed me as triumphs of gastronomy and, with anything more modest, I think it's a pity to mix the two great red wines at the same meal. The Burgundy should appeal to the senses, the claret may well attract the attention of the mind. It's rather like trying to enjoy a claret that offers Mozart or Bach in the first part, Wagner or Sibelius after! If you wish, try – and take a matured claret to put against a red Burgundy. But, because of the changes in vintages that are bound to occur, you should take the advice of a merchant about the pair of wines to select. The Cape wine is a charming introductory drink before the rather 'important' bottles to follow. Notice the relief of Table Mountain on the back of the dumpy bottle, rising above the vineyards. Be careful, with the Cuvée Latour, that no one ever gets confused between Louis Latour, this great Burgundy establishment, and Château Latour, the first growth of Pauillac in the Médoc in the Bordeaux region. The two wines of the Hautes Côtes (literally 'higher slopes') of Beaune and Nuits are the sort of Burgundies that are both affordable and, thanks to modern methods of cultivation and production, both enjoyable and, when from reputable establishments, true small-scale Burgundies.

Bellingham Cape Gold

This is one of the most beautiful properties, the lovely house being most carefully enhanced and the garden landscaped by the present owners; you can see the front of the house on the label.

The colour: Lemon-lime, almost greenish.

The smell: Fresh, slightly of clean vegetation.

The flavour: Light, rounded, fruity, eminently pleasant for anytime drinking and, as here, for an interesting and clean 'mouth wash'.

Cuvée Latour, 1982, Louis Latour

This wine, bearing only the modest A.C. 'Bourgogne' is composed by this famous Burgundy house from the wines of rather more 'quality' vineyards than you might suppose from the label. The blend varies a little from year to year, for obvious reasons, but the only grape used is the Chardonnay, the great white grape that makes all the finest white Burgundies and that wins admiration for the wines it makes all round the world.

The colour: A definite light gold, with a touch of paleness at the rim.

The smell: Very assertive – almost piercing. I once described a typical Chardonnay smell as a 'rapier'.

The flavour: Medium full, vigorous but quite elegant, with an underlying firmness and fair length. A practical point – if you are showing a Chardonnay wine together with wines from other grapes, show the Chardonnay last – unless the other wines are far superior quality, the Chardonnay will overwhelm them. You might care to compare this with Beaujolais Blanc of Session 16 which is, also made from the Chardonnay, but slightly more to the south.

Hautes Côtes de Beaune Villages 1982, Delamont

This region is south-west of Beaune and is now being extensively planted with the quality grapes, whereas, until fairly recently, growers concentrated on high yields rather than fine wines. Mostly red wine is made here, the small amount of white usually being drunk locally. The 'Villages' are a group allowed to use this A.O.C.

The colour: A rosy-red, with a blueish rim – the wine is still fairly young and there isn't much overall shading anyway.

The smell: Very much 'cassis', the blackcurrant fragrance that is associated with the Pinot Noir, the sole black grape that makes fine red Burgundy.

The flavour: The wine was still young when I tasted it, but it is taut, well 'together' and agreeably fresh – the sort of Burgundy that makes most agreeable drinking for formal or informal occasions and is in no way like the souped-up treacly vulgar red wines that some people associate with the great wine region and that have, in the past, been made by unscrupulous firms pandering to the public's love of the name Burgundy.

Hautes Côtes de Nuits Villages 1979, Joseph Drouhin

This is an older wine, which may not always be available; choose either two reds of the same vintage or, as here, one slightly older. Wines of this A.C. are unlikely to age quite as long as those with the most distinguished A.C.s of the Côtes de Beaune and Côtes de Nuits (the two regions that make up the Côtes d'Or, Burgundy's 'golden slope'), but they are usually good for several years if correctly stored. This vineyard area is smaller than that of the previous red Burgundy but, like that one, a number of villages here have the right to add this A.O.C. to their wines. White – Aligoté – and Gamay wines, also rosé wines are made in this area, which is on the slopes above the main Côte de Nuits, where the very finest red Burgundies are made.

The colour: Very shaded – the sample tried here was after all old – with a tawny tone apparent at the edge of the wine, where it meets the glass.

The smell: Very definitely Pinot Noir, though not quite as obviously 'cassis' as the younger wine. The fresh, soft, waft of aroma is velvety and welcoming – although, to be fair, all good Burgundy should also have that slightly vegetative smell: indeed, one great authority says definitely, 'Good Burgundy smells of shit.' If it reminds you, agreeably of course, of the farmyard, so much the better!

The flavour: This is also very typical red Burgundy – giving an initial impression of softness, but with good underlying 'bone structure', so that the wine, gentle as it seems at first, is really quite firm and almost gutsy, leaving the palate with a defined taste that is rather elegant.

Alternatives: You could limit this session only to the Burgundies, but the Cape wine provides a pleasant introduction – some people may find the Chardonnay rather too 'big' and uncompromisingly dry, which it should be. White Mâcon, from the Chardonnay, and Pouilly Fuissé likewise, are possible but not necessarily to the taste of everybody. If you wish, try as substitutes Chardonnay wines from other countries – those of Australia and New Zealand are most interesting, often showing what I frequently note as a 'buttery', almost fat fragrance and taste. California Chardonnays can be a bit obviously 'wooded' – the grape takes on so much of the wood in which it has been matured that if this is carried to what a European might find excessive lengths, the wine can seem top heavy. As far as the red wines are concerned, again you can find Pinot Noir wines from many countries, but, if you want to learn about red Burgundy, it's worth keeping within the region: from the south of the area you can find the red wines of Mâcon, or, more importantly, those of Mercurey, Givry, Rully, as yet undeservedly little-known, but much appreciated as small-scale and reasonably priced (just) Burgundies for the more knowing.

Conclusion: Burgundy, because of the complexity of the Appellation Contrôlée controls, the splitting up of the vineyards among many owners, and the different styles of wine made by growers and shippers, is not an easy wine to know overall. To get quality, one must be prepared to pay and to be sure of 'real' Burgundy of traditional style, one must take the trouble to find out the names of respected shippers (growers' wines may be really expensive) and note the differences in the sorts of wines each will make. Never risk the 'doubtful bargain' as far as Burgundy is concerned and, if possible, take advice before you buy. It is one of the greatest wines in the world, but it's truly said that, as far as the very finest wines are concerned, you'll be lucky (however much money you have) if you can drink a top Burgundy once or twice a year, whereas (if you can afford it) you might easily drink a top claret once or twice a week!

Suggested food: Burgundian fare is rich – it isn't by chance that the peasant is often the pear shape of the top of the Burgundy bottle! A real Burgundy dinner might start with the raw ham for which Morvan is famous, or eggs poached in red wine with a shallot sauce, or jambon persillé, the special ham in parsley-flavoured jelly, or of course, the fat Burgundian snails with garlic butter. One could then – if stalwart – go on to boeuf à la Bourguignonne, a beef stew, or 'chicken in half mourning', which is chicken with its breast threaded with black truffles, proceed to a salad and cheese, and then a blackcurrant (cassis) sorbet, with the cassis liqueur poured over the top. A less gastronomically and financially taxing menu could begin with some form of raw ham with melon, or eggs in a wine-flavoured aspic, sitting on a chunk of mousse de foie de volaille or good chicken paté and topped with a little chopped ham. Then you could have the Burgundian coq au vin – using some of the red wine for the recipe; don't get any old cheap red for this, as a good but not extra-fine red Burgundy really does make the dish better. In season, this is a very good menu for jugged hare, or a casserole of rabbit or pigeon. Then, after some creamy cheese with which to finish the wine, you could have a blackcurrant ice or blackcurrant sponge pudding or tart. For a really simple but excellent meal, try a starter of cold scrambled eggs with chopped mushrooms, or a fish pâté followed by either black pudding ('boudin') with potato pureé and apples cooked lightly in butter, or several meat, poultry and game pâtés or forms of sausage, with a mixed green salad – plus garlic croûtons if you know everyone likes the flavour. End with baked apples and tip some of the white wine into each before cooking.

146

W   I   N   E   S

1 Gisborne 1982 Gewurztraminer, Cook's New Zealand
Wine Company
2 1982 Gewurztraminer d'Alsace, Louis Gisselbrecht
3 1980 Torres Coroñas.

Availability: Cullens

Theme: Registering the Gewurztraminer grape and a fine Spanish wine from a region other than Rioja.

Practicalities: Chill the two white wines an hour in the refrigerator or in a deep bucket of ice and water for fifteen minutes. Draw the cork on the Coroñas an hour ahead of drinking time, or, if you wish, decant this fine wine in advance.

What you're aiming to do: The Gewurztraminer grape is very much the 'when-in-doubt' choice on many occasions, because its spiciness enables it to go with food, also to provide a substantial drink as an apéritif. The two white wines show how a New World vineyard can produce a baby classic and how Alsace provides fine wine from this grape. The Coroñas is a wine from the hinterland of Barcelona – totally different from Rioja. It is made by someone I consider to be one of the great wine makers of the world.

Talking points: Although New Zealand has been making wine – and even attracting the praise of visiting Frenchmen! – since the first part of the nineteenth century, even winning awards at international competitions in Europe, it's only recently that wine has become big business there. New Zealand wines are not like Australian wines (the country and climate are quite different) and at present it's probably the whites, drunk in huge amounts in their homeland, that tend to appeal most easily. Cook's set up their installations in the 1970s and have made steady progress, with vineyards in various regions of the North Island; this one comes from Gisborne, south of Auckland, on the east coast. The spicy Traminer (the translation of 'Gewurztraminer') originated in the Palatinate or Pfalz region of Germany; it's a wine that appeals enormously on account of its aroma.

The Alsace wine comes from a fine maker at Dambach-la-Ville, an attractive little wine village along the 'Wine Road'.

Miguel Torres Junior, who made the Coroñas, is the wine maker of a much respected and long-established wine family at Vilafranca del Penedés, in the north-east of Spain. This, until 1714, was part of the old Kingdom of Catalunya and is rich in works of art and good, fine and peasanty fare, as well as making many wines, including vast quantities of sparkling wines. But the Torres family (who've now bought a property in Chile) make only still wine and brandy. Their wines have won awards all over the world and are much sought-after in the US as well as in Britain.

TASTING NOTES

Cooks 1982 Gewurztraminer

The back label gives a lot of information – the southern hemisphere drinkers like many details about the production of their wines to be included. Essentially, this is a very well-made wine, a little less sure of itself than the Alsace, but no less charming for that, the product of an accomplished wine maker who has, even while young, won many awards.

The colour: Light gold, no sign of shading.

The smell: Rather delicate (as compared with a European Gewurztraminer), but there is the whiff of cool, spicy fragrance.

The flavour: It slides very easily across the palate and is a surprisingly big-bodied wine, evocative of sun and open spaces. Perhaps it's a little 'short' and waves goodbye to the palate rather briskly? But it's a delicious mouthful while it lasts. Later vintages may be slightly different.

Louis Giselbrecht 1982 Gewurztraminer

This vintage was a huge one in Alsace and this maker, always very elegant and careful to make well-proportioned wines, has kept this example very much in trim. An Alsace Gewurztraminer is definitely the wine to go with all sorts of food, if people are not sure whether they really like a very dry wine; the grape is cultivated in Germany, but it seems to give of its best in Alsace. A 1983 will be bigger and more important.

The colour: Deeper than the New Zealand wine and a definite gold, though not darkening because of any age as yet.

The smell: Spice – but with great freshness. Try to register the spice you first think of – cinnamon? Nutmeg? Even a whiff of cloves? To me this aroma is usually evocative of hay freshly cut, probably with some flowers in it – of course, hay and flowers mightn't smell at all like that if I stuck my nose into them, but in my mind this is what the Gewurztraminer conjures up.

The flavour: This is definitely a dry wine, in spite of the big bouquet. There's a firm, inner core of close-knit strands of taste that are fascinating to sample and then, as you drink or swallow, the wine developes a crescendo of flavour, lingering long in the mouth. Yet, all the while, it is fresh and never cloys or assaults the palate – its style is elegant and completely well-bred.

1980 Torres Coronas

The back label of this wine gives detailed information about it – but remember, you don't *have* to agree with the opinions! The Torres range of wines includes some beauties, but this is a very good example of a wine that has a wide appeal and yet is adaptable to formal or casual food. The use of two grape varieties (Ull de Liebre and Monastrell) peculiar to the Penedés region is interesting, but Miguel Torres, who has trained and studied in France and travelled the world, has also made wines using other classic and well-known wine grapes (all of those you'll have studied in these sessions) so all his wines are worth exploring.

The colour: Very shaded, from an extremely dark central point out to an almost purple-blue rim.

The smell: There is a very creamy, almost fat smell that I often pick up from the Ull de Liebre – a rich, inviting bouquet.

The flavour: Note the fine proportions of this wine – the balance of fruit, acidity and, at the back of it all and unable to be tasted, the alcohol that holds everything together like a human's skeleton. This wine welcomes the drinker, but doesn't rush to make an impression. It lingers gently on the palate, inviting you to sample it again.

Conclusion: To limit oneself to European wines is to deprive the wine lover of much pleasure, and it can be exciting and illuminating when one sees how good many wines from 'new' regions can be. Spain isn't only Rioja nor need wines made in the New World from classic grapes fear comparison with European wines based on the same grapes these days.

Alternatives: There are a number of New Zealand wines coming into the UK these days, so you may be able to find another Gewurztraminer. There are numerous Alsace wines made from this grape, each individual according to the maker. As far as the Coroñas is concerned, an equivalent is impossible, although these days there are several other firms from the Penedés region making very good wines and sending some to the UK.

Suggested food: The New Zealand wine could be the apéritif, then, with a first course partnered by the Alsace, you could have some pâté or a salady dish, or, if you feel like showing-off, a cheese soufflé or cheese and tomato croustades – on toast. The main dish could be at least vaguely Catalan, such as any of the country recipes involving beans, sausages and pork or chicken – your own adaptation of a cassoulet perhaps, or a beanpot. Afterwards perhaps a melon stuffed with fresh fruit – save a little of the Alsace to pour into this and sip with it, if you don't want to serve a sweet wine. A more straightforward menu could be shrimps or shellfish to eat with your fingers, duckling with orange sauce, or a pork casserole, and kiwi fruit to conclude. But if you can offer a few different cold cuts and sausages, plus cheese, especially goat and ewe cheese, with some fresh fruit, you have a perfectly adequate meal.

W	I	N	E	S

1 Verdicchio dei Castelli di Jesi 1983
2 Grunberger Stein
3 Rosemount Estate Cabernet Sauvignon 1980
4 KWV Golden Vintage 1981

Availability: Victoria Wine

Theme: Why the same wine from a different source must be different; two wines to introduce a fine New World Cabernet Sauvignon.

Practicalities: Chill the Verdicchio, the Grunberger Stein and the Golden Vintage either for an hour in the refrigerator or a quarter of an hour in a deep bucket of ice and water. The Verdicchio is the apéritif, the Golden Vintage for serving at the end of the meal, so this can be left in to go on chilling, unless it's a very cold day. Draw the cork on the Rosemount at least an hour – preferably two – before you are going to pour it or, ideally, decant it at least an hour beforehand; this is a very fine wine and merits such attention. If you don't feel up to serving four wines, then select one of the first two whites – the Verdicchio is drier than the Grunberger and indeed the Grunberger is virtually an anytime agreeable drink. But it provides an alternative white choice for people who may find the Rosemount too imposing for their particular taste and who like a touch of softness about white wines.

What you're aiming to do: One wine isn't like another – even when it bears the same name. This Verdicchio is very different in character from that of Session 7. Keep an open mind about all wines and, if you particularly like the wine from one maker or shipper, make a note of this, just any old wine of the same name may disappoint you. The Grunberger is a very amiable wine, multi-purpose and not well known in the UK. The Golden Vintage is a delicious drink – try to compare it with some of the other sweetish wines (Session 4 and 6) and to make a crisp sweetish wine in the hot vineyards of the Cape is a triumph of the maker's art. The Rosemount not only displays the Cabernet Sauvignon at its best, but is another triumph for the maker – it comes from the Hunter River region of New South Wales where, as some of the wine producers say, 'God didn't mean vines to grow'. Rosemount has been winning medals and prizes all over its homeland and the world, although it's a newish concern. You'll see why its reputation is very high.

Talking points: It's always interesting to plan a set of wines around one that's outstanding – which is why the white wines are a little lower in key. You may or may not like the Rosemount, rather depending on whether you like quality Cabernet Sauvignon wines; you're unlikely to be unaware of a very special style. If you wish, you could cut all but one white wine – for apéritif and first course – and put another straight Cabernet into this session (see Session 14). This may not be to the taste of everybody, but it can be a delight to some wine lovers who appreciate claret. Or, as an introductory red, try the Stellenberg Roodekeur, a Cape wine from the coastal region, very soft and warm, also from Victoria Wine.

TASTING NOTES

Verdicchio dei Castelli di Jesi 1983

This is a dry, fairly crisp wine, but quite different from that of Session 7.

The colour: Yellow-toned, verging on gold.

The smell: The Trebbiano Toscano grape gives this a touch of vanilla and a very light spice to the smell, but this is not pronounced – remember, the Italian preference is for wines that are not too obvious in bouquet.

The flavour: Round, quite fat in its initial impact on the palate, then it finishes definitely dry.

Grunberger Stein

Don't let the flagon-shaped bottle and the word 'Stein' – which means 'stone' – confuse you into linking this wine with the Franconian 'Steinwein', from Germany, which can also come in a dumpy bottle, known as a Boxbeutel. This Cape wine is quite different.

The colour: Fairly definite lemon.

The smell: A waft of slight sweetness and the honeyed fragrance of the Chenin Blanc (see Session 9).

The flavour: This is described as 'semi-sweet' but in fact it ends neatly and almost dry, so that it leaves the palate fresh and clean.

Rosemount Cabernet Sauvignon 1980

Rosemount Estate is in the upper Hunter Valley of New South Wales. This is impressive wine country with fine estates – but for many reasons it isn't ideal for vines and wine growers in other regions tend to say, 'Only once in seven years for the Hunter.' Rosemount Estate has been under vines since the turn of the century, but a dynamic set of new owners in the early 1970s has made the Rosemount wines world-famous – they make wine in other Australian wine areas now as well. The winning of awards makes national front page news in Australia and judging is severe – think of appraising several hundred different wines in a day!

The colour: Still very dark and note the many different colour tones. It's a deep plum red, with a touch of purple, the rim of the wine being almost blue.

The smell: Straightforward Cabernet Sauvignon – the firm, leafy freshness, direct impression on the nose.

The flavour: This wine is far from its prime as I write about it and it has the reserve of really fine red wines – always alluring the drinker to take another sip and perhaps discover some additional attribute and pleasure! It's full, but not aggressive, there's plenty of fruit to the taste but note the astringency of the tannin underlying this – indicative of a long life. There's a lingering impression after you've swallowed it – of a firm, full, ripe wine of the great Cabernet Sauvignon. 'Huff' air down your nose and out of your mouth after swallowing to get the full effect of the after-taste – it reveals more refinement and complexity, indicative of what sort of qualities the wine may develop. It's because of the reserve of this wine that it should if possible be opened well in advance or decanted, so that the aeration can open it up and bring it on.

KWV Golden Vintage 1981

This is from the coastal region of the Cape and is a vintage – the two coloured bands indicate this. It's made from fully ripe, almost overripe grapes, by the KWV, the huge wine co-operative in Paarl, whose wines are produced at levels of quality to impress the most demanding wine makers of the world who visit the enormous installations.

The colour: Definite gold, lightening a little at the rim.

The smell: Sunny, warm, but with a freshing additional whiff of something my notes put down as '? apple mint'. This is up to you to define.

The flavour: Full, but with a definite cool freshness underneath the sunny taste that gives the wine agreeable balance and zip – you could in fact enjoy it at almost any time as well as at the end of a meal. It's a 'smiling wine' and although vigorously honeyed, it has a crisp finish.

Conclusion: Any fine and important wine deserves to have the other wines around it 'programmed' to set it off. This is why the whites at the outset are generally agreeable, dry and slightly sweet, working up to the fine Cabernet Sauvignon. The Golden Vintage is a totally different type of wine, sufficiently well made not to be an anti-climax after the Rosemount, but providing charm and amiability as a contrast.

Alternatives: Difficult to find an equivalent to the Rosemount, but there are plenty of excellent Australian Cabernet Sauvignons available – try one from the curious Coonawarra region (Rosemount make one there too) in South Australia, or perhaps a California Cabernet. With the last, however, don't get too cheap a wine – you will inevitably pay for the quality and the exchange rate may be against you. Try another Verdicchio – you could put two side by side if you like to compare differences – and you could have a late-picked Cape Chenin Blanc for the Golden Vintage. As has been suggested, you can put other Cabernets into this progression of wines, but be careful not to put an old wine in front of a young one, as if you do the younger wine may not be as attractive as it otherwise would. If you wish, try a 1980 red Bordeaux alongside the Rosemount, but the clarets of this vintage were not as imposing as the Australian wine – if you want to end with a claret, try something older, bearing in mind that often New World wines do 'come on' to maturity slightly more quickly than those of some vintages of Bordeaux.

Suggested food: If possible, this Cabernet deserves something rather good – grilled steak or perhaps a joint of lamb. You could plan the meal around a roast chicken (not too much sage in any stuffing), or a steak and mushroom pie, or simply cold roast beef with baked potatoes. Possible starters include tomatoes stuffed with rice and shrimps, a 'tart' of fonds d'artichauts, or simply a salad of white fish, with a light lemony mayonnaise or sauce verte. You should certainly try to have some creamy cheese to finish the red wine and then the sweet wine can accompany a trifle, crème caramel or any sponge pudding or sponge and jam sandwich cake.

The Cabernet Sauvignon is so famous and esteemed that it's worth trying as many examples as possible. You should get additional substitutes from the more expensive wines – but remember they do need care in handling. Their imposing style is rewarding but, for some people, the dryness and uncompromising character is not always easily liked. Red Bordeaux (Session 4) includes this grape plus others, but you can find wines from the grape from all over the world. Respect them.

W	I	N	E	S

1 1984 Old Triangle Vineyard, Barossa Valley Riesling,
   Hill-Smith Estate, Angaston, South Australia
2 1977 Viña Undurraga Santa Ana, Pinot Noir, Chile

Availability: Cullens

Theme: A Rheinriesling from the southern hemisphere and a
red from ungrafted vine stocks to impress even the most
chauvinistic visiting Frenchman!

Practicalities: Cool the Riesling for an hour in the refrigerator
or just about fifteen minutes in a deep bucket of ice and water.
Draw the cork on the Pinot Noir an hour before you want to
pour it. If possible, for any foreign visitor, I'd like to suggest
you offer an English dry white wine as the apéritif – there are
plenty about these days, but, as quantities made at any one
time can be limited, it's up to you to look out for something of
this kind. Go for the light whites, possibly noting those made
from the Müller-Thurgau grape or the hybrid, Seyval Blanc,
but there are many others.

What you're aiming to do: Nothing is more unwise than to
suppose you really *do* know and can recognise a wine. You may
be able to do so, but some of the greatest tasters have been
mistaken and, if one wishes, it's always possible, by choosing
certain wines, to mislead the arrogant. However, this isn't
civilised – everyone can and does make mistakes. What you're
doing in this session is to register a white wine from Australia
that's so fresh and crisp it's difficult to understand how it can
come from a fairly warm vineyard. The red wine, from Chile,
is very unusual, because this country has virtually no virus

diseases and the phylloxera, the aphis that destroys vine roots, never got there, so none of the vines have had to be grafted onto resistant rootstocks. This means that such 'national' vines are of great interest – demonstrating that this is the style of wine our ancestors might have drunk, had they known as much about wine making as is known today. Chile is of enormous interest because of this, although there are some patches of ungrafted vines in parts of Australia, New Zealand, Portugal and Hungary. It seems to me that there is a slight difference in the overall character of wines from such vines. Anyway, it's wonderful to try them. Chile makes many wines from classic grapes and I was very tempted to put in a Cabernet Sauvignon as well, but Cullens, who have a very wide range of Chilean wines, stock plenty from different wineries, so you can add to the selection if you wish.

Talking points: The Barossa Valley, north-east of Adelaide in South Australia, is lovely, rolling countryside. Many Germans settled there in the early days and there was even a local German dialect, as well as many foods and traditions showing German influence, such as vintage carnivals, brass bands and many huge, impressive installations. The fresh, cool climate of the uplands enables crisp white wines to be made, although virtually every sort of wine is produced, in vast amounts. The Hill-Smith family firm, whose premises are shown on the label, although the country house where they live is, as it were, out of the picture, can now chalk up six generations in the business and their wines are world-respected, notably the Rieslings. The Undurraga installations are both traditional and impressive: on the label you see the curious country house of the founders of the firm, incorporating many sorts of architectural style and standing in a beautiful garden. The installations themselves are picturesque, with huge wooden casks and roof beams, but impeccably clean and, today, scientific methods are assisting old-style wine making (Miguel Torres has been influential in Chile as well). But don't overlook any of the Chilean firms exporting to the UK, their red wines are of enormous interest and, in a recent very high-powered tasting at a London club, with expensive wines tasted blind, it was the cheapest, from Chile, that got top marks!

1984 Old Triangle Vineyard Barossa Valley Riesling, Hill-Smith estate

It's a test of the wine maker's ability to make a crisp, fresh white wine in a warm vineyard. Luckily, here there's sufficient altitude and plenty of know-how. Anyone supposing that 'Aussie' wines lack delicacy will have to swallow their words after this one!

The colour: Pale lemon, with a hint of lime green.

The smell: The nobility of the Riesling is here – slightly subdued (but the sample when tasted was only recently bottled and a mere five months old), but fresh, very much the 'cool breeze off an upland meadow' smell, that I sometimes note over a wine I particularly like made from this grape. 'Mountain flowers' is often said of the Riesling d'Alsace (see Session 2).

The flavour: Quite a big wine, rounded, moderately assertive and, although flowing smoothly over the palate, establishing itself as a fruity, noble product of the Riesling.

1977 Undurraga Santa Ana Pinot Noir

This is bottled in a dumpy bottle that was originally used to distinguish this winery's products, but is now established as a favourite anyway. It derives from the Franconian 'Steinwein' boxbeutel, but in Chile it is known as a 'Caramayola'. If you get a slightly more recent vintage, don't worry too much – vintages in this beautiful country do not vary a great deal, although naturally the wines change as they age.

The colour: A deep, fairly shaded wine, with a pale edge. A plum-rhododendron tone – the Pinot Noir red is usually quite different from the red imparted by the pigments on the skins of the Cabernet Sauvignon, and Pinot Noir lightens to pale pinkish-blue, rather than tawny.

The smell: Lovely 'dust and leaves' fragrance – the sort of smell you inhale when, in a town, there's a brief shower and you breathe the freshness of the pavements and suburban garden shrubs. Compare this soft smell with the more definite blackcurrant smell of the Burgundy Pinot Noir (Session 17).

The flavour; Soft, shy – it comes hesitantly into the mouth and seems quite light in body – until you realise that it has opened out on the palate both discreetly and impressively and then the taste becomes full and almost sweet, except that there is certainly no sort of sweetening to this wine apart from the natural grape sugar. Do you seem to be able to plunge into the taste? That is what I term 'depth' in a wine – one goes down into different layers of flavour. It may be imagination, but red wines from ungrafted classic wine grapes always seem to·me to possess this soft but powerful deep style.

Alternatives: There are many Australian Rieslings, from the various wine regions of this enormous country, but check before you buy that you get the true Rheinriesling. Some other Chilean wineries produce Pinot Noir, but if you want a real contrast, then go for a Pinot Noir from a fairly cool country – the New Zealand wines from this grape are as yet in their infancy, but they may be suitable. The Pinot Noir likes a fairly low temperature, which is why Chile, where it drops sharply at night, is a good vineyard for it. Try the Torres wines from Chile when they are available.

Conclusions: One should always keep an open mind about wine! New techniques, wine makers who may infuriate their colleagues and, simply, new business ventures can all make it possible for wines to be made where they couldn't previously have been made. With bottling, stabilising and transport facilities, wines can come from the other side of the world to delight even the most severe taster.

Suggested food: Suppose you're offering an English wine as apéritif, serve cheese straws or canapés of the creamiest British cheese you can find – the hard cheeses tend to be too strong for this type of wine. Then you can start the meal with potted shrimps or small portions of smoked salmon kedgeree. Go on to steak, kidney and mushroom pie, hot or cold, with vegetables in season, followed by summer pudding or maids of honour or, in winter, any traditional steamed pudding.

THREE BUFFET PARTIES

Entertaining is very much up to you these days. But the buffet or version of a self-service light meal, plus a selection of wines, is definitely popular. There are cheese and wine parties, salad selection parties, quiche parties, sausage and salami parties, pâté parties – you think of the food and it's the basis for an informal gathering.

It adds to the interest if you have more than, say, white and red wine to accompany the fare, so here are three ways in which you can extend your tasting experience and, certainly, provide an opportunity for friends to compare several wines at a time when sampling different dishes. These sessions have not been linked to any single retail outlet, because the wines are widely available and although they may vary a little, you will be able to appreciate the various styles of the separate categories.

Although all the wines will be perfectly suited to most buffet food, go easy on anything with curry, or any very piquant salad dressings, and it's difficult to taste most wines against pineapple – and impossible against chocolate! These are not very serious tasting sessions, but, for those of you and your friends who always enjoy learning something from the wines you drink, the use of several bottles for such occasions can be a pleasant enhancement of hospitality. Don't forget that many of the firms mentioned in this book can arrange to lend you glasses for a minimum charge and that, if you're ordering the wine, most will accept an order on 'sale or return' terms, which means that you only pay for the bottles you actually consume. (Though don't damage the labels or remove the capsules.)

THE PINK PARTY –

WITH VIN ROSÉ

Our Edwardian forbears were fond of giving parties where everything, food, drink, tableware and décor, was all one colour. It can be a pretty idea with fresh, light colours, but you needn't be too conscientious about making all the food pink for a vin rosé session. One of the most attractive summer buffets

I've seen was in the garden of a dedicated rose grower – a rose of approximately the same colour as the vin rosé was arranged in a glass at each tasting table.

Most vin rosé is non-vintage, ready to enjoy when bottled. It should be served chilled, so have plenty of ice buckets – filled with ice and water, not ice alone – and napkins to stop the cold water dripping onto the food. As pink wine of quality gets its colour from the pigments in the skins of black grapes, which are allowed to remain in contact with the freshly pressed juice until they tint it, there's a huge range of different tones of pink. In southern vineyards, such as those of the Rhône Valley, a pink wine – the most famous is Tavel – may be quite deep rose. This will be more expensive. There are not so many in the southern hemisphere, although some are made in South Africa. Italian rosati are made in many regions, especially Sardinia; in Cyprus there are full-bodied versions, verging into red in colour. The Corsican rosés are usually good, also full-bodied and aromatic. The famous Rosé d'Anjou is a more brilliant sharp pink. Mateus Rosé, perhaps the most famous pink wine in the world, is a light, fresh rosy wine, with a hint of the bronze-pink of its Portuguese homeland, while the rosado wines of Spain are inclined to be more definitely rose pink, with often a slight golden shade apparent if you look closely at the glass tilted over something white.

The colour: The further north the vineyard, the lighter the tone. The pigments in some grapes grown in warm southern vineyards can make certain vin rosé wines almost light-tone reds – anyone who knows Cyprus will appreciate this. Some of the southern rosés, too, have a touch of orange or light flame in their pinkness.

The smell: All rosé should smell fresh, but some are fruitier than others. You will probably get an impression of a young wine, which may be varied as to its crispness or fullness. It won't be particularly complex, it should invite you to drink.

The flavour: This naturally depends on the wine, but in general a lightish, agreeable taste is what the makers of rosé aim at. There should be a little fruit, sometimes a touch of sweetness. The overall impression should be agreeable, clean – and 'more-ish'.

Conclusion: Select your rosé from as wide a range as possible. You'll pay more for Tavel and probably more for a Rosé d'Anjou than just 'French rosé', but the difference between the wines will be apparent. Don't suppose that vin rosé will go with *any* cold food, it's never intended for partnering very full-flavoured dishes, but can be excellent with many fish and shellfish dishes, vegetable pâté, chicken and ham pie, cold chicken and many forms of quiche.

THE BUBBLY PARTY –

WITH SPARKLING WINE

This is a party that will always be enjoyed – sparkling wine gives an atmosphere of celebration from the outset! But it also provides a useful way of learning about different sparklers, so that, should you only want a single bottle at some time, you'll have a notion as to the type you will do well to buy.

There are three main methods of making a wine sparkling, but the one that utilises the pumping in of gas is not able to make more than a lighthearted 'fun' wine and so the two principal procedures are those that are called 'cuve close' or 'sealed vat' and the Champagne process, for wines other than those made in the Champagne region. Champagne method wines take longer to produce and involve more detailed skill – so they are more expensive; but, in certain areas, they are very good indeed. The Loire Champagne method wines, for example, of which Saumur is very well known, are excellent in quality and good value; Blanquette de Limoux, from the south-east corner of France, is proud of being able to consider itself the oldest sparkling wine of its kind – the makers claim they evolved the process for their wines before Dom Pérignon! In Spain, huge amounts of sparklers are made by the Champagne process: in and around Barcelona. For example, they'll drink this type of wine often in preference to sherry (which comes from the south). Waiters will refer to 'Champaña', but they should say 'Espumoso', because since 1973 there's been a legal decree between France and Spain restricting the use of 'Champagne' only to the wine of the north of France, grown and made in the Champagne district. The word 'cava' on a Spanish sparkling wine means that it will have been produced according to the Champagne method.

The 'cuve close' or 'sealed vat' method was evolved commercially by the man who made the first Veuve du Vernay, the top selling sparkler. Essentially, this by-passes the complex stages whereby Champagne spends most of its life in bottle, being matured and carefully handled throughout. For a 'cuve close' wine the length of time involved is not so great – nor would the wine benefit if longer time were taken, so this is an economy. The wine spends most of its life in a vat, sealed at the top so that the fizz can't get out, hence the name 'sealed vat'. The seal on the vat acts in the same way as the cork in the bottle in the Champagne process – it seals in the effervescence.

With world demand for sparkling wines increasing – and the price of Champagne unlikely to drop, alas! – sparkling wines are made in many countries. One of the most famous is Italy's Asti Spumante, produced by an adroit combination of some of the procedures followed in the 'sealed vat' method; the basic method had to be modified, because the natural sugar in the Moscato grape – making very fruity wines – accentuates the pressure in the bottle so much so that, in former times, explosions and loss of wine were serious.

Basic tasting standards: Judging a quality sparkling wine is not difficult – examine it for colour, smell and flavour just as you would a still wine. You should also note the 'mousse' or fizz, because a good sparkler should have plenty of tiny bubbles, which rise fast and go on rising for quite a time. Of course, glasses must be free from grease or detergent, even the use of detergent not well rinsed from a drying cloth may affect the glass and the best sparkler may go flat quickly and disappoint the drinker.

When arranging sparkling wines, put the sweeter examples after the dry ones. The word 'Brut' on a label means dry. Among the great Spanish establishments making these wines there will often be several of different qualities – you will note this by the price. Here 'secco' also means dry. Some of the white sparkling wines of the Loire vary in sweetness as well as in the different styles made by the many establishments; here, the term 'demi sec' usually means sweet – as it does on the labels of other French sparkling wines. In Germany, 'sekt' is the term usually applied to sparkling wines, but, although these are mostly fairly dry, the term 'sekt' doesn't necessarily mean dry, so look for other indications on labels. The term 'blanc de blancs' merely means 'a white wine made from white grapes' but many of the grapes used for sparkling wines are white anyway, so this is rather a meaningless phrase, although label designers often suppose it to convey some cachet on the wine.

Remember that sometimes a sparkling wine will be made in a dry and a sweet version (Veuve du Vernay, for example), so make sure you get the one you want. Also, most of the large-scale retailers tend to have their own brands of sparkling wines – their own Asti, Saumur, 'French sparkling' and so on. Because these will be bought in huge quantities and do not have to bear the costs of general advertising, like a national brand, they may offer a decided saving in overall cost. Don't think that they are 'less good' – they may be very good indeed!

Practicalities: Sparkling wine should always be served cold, but not iced, so plunge the bottles up to their necks in a mixture of ice and water for a quarter of an hour, or put them in the refrigerator for an hour. If they are really icy cold, they will not yield their smell (which you've paid for) and can also lack much of their taste.

When opening any sparkling wine, remember to hold the bottle with a cloth – it's rare these days that a bottle splits, but it can happen and then a serious injury can result. Also, once you've removed the 'muzzle' of wire, *don't let go of the cork* for an instant! It may seem stuck – but it can come out like a bullet and every year many people lose an eye because either someone aims the bottle at their face or when opening, somebody leaves go of the cork and looks down at it. Great care must *always* be observed when opening any sparkling wine and, of course, *never* use a gas cork extractor, which can make the bottle explode. Always have glasses to hand when opening the bottle, so that you don't waste any of the wine, it can never be cheap. Try to get the cork out only making a discreet 'burp'; to 'pop' a cork and let it fly is not only potentially dangerous, it really isn't the way to serve a good wine.

Suggested wines: Veuve du Vernay (dry); a 'cava' wine from Spain, non-vintage: Codorniu, Freixenet and Monistrol all make good wines of this type; a sparkling wine from the Loire – many firms have a Saumur; Asti Spumante – the same applies here, it's widely on sale.

Possible alternatives – or additions: A sekt (Blue Nun comes in a sparkling version), possibly Blanquette de Limoux, stocked by quite a number of outlets; a French sparkling wine from another region than the Loire, or Limoux (there are plenty) or from South Africa (the KWV make a pleasing sparkler). Otherwise, if you can range around and perhaps consult a specialist retailer, you may be able to find sparkling Burgundy, white and red (though this is a little full for very casual drinking); the 'mad' sparkling wine of the Jura, vin fou; a very fine California wine called Schramsburg and so on, virtually ad infinitum. Or simply select a brand you don't know of a wine you already like and see if your first preference is still sound.

Suggested food: Sparkling wine is very good with light, elegant snacks, but can also stand up to more robust fare: mayonnaise and eggy, creamy sauces for meat, poultry and fish. It is also excellent with certain veal and cream recipes, good with most smoked fish – and, of course, with oysters and caviare, although these luxuries really merit the supreme sparkler, Champagne. However, with shellfish and lumpfish roe a good sparkler is very good. If you can, reserve most examples of Asti for such delights as pastries, ices and fruit and cream, although it can be pleasant with some salads, pâtés and quiches, where a very grapey wine is a suitable partner.

THE CHAMPAGNE PARTY

This is not only the most luxurious of drinks, and likely to be the most esteemed in terms of celebration, but in fact it can be the most rewarding in tasting terms too. For Champagne isn't 'just Champagne'. As with all fine wines, its different wines possess marked individuality. Even within the same price range you'll notice tremendous differences; if you taste a good wine against a great one you'll be astonished. You may end by liking the good (and cheaper) wine better, but you'll appreciate the details of quality that can make one non-vintage Champagne twice the price of another. It might make a memorable conclusion for the friends with whom you've been tasting to hold a Champagne session, or you can simply arrange this as a preliminary to a wedding, anniversary, birthday or similar special occasion. But not just because the Champagnes are expensive, but because they are fine wines, don't be shy about taking a little trouble to present them – and knowing how to point out to the discriminating the difference between one wine and another.

It's assumed that, if you're into vintage Champagnes, or, certainly, the luxury blends, you'll already have some knowledge of the wine. Here, I suggest a comparison of non-vintage Champagnes – all delicious, each individual. Bear in mind that a world-famous and well-advertised 'marque' or particular wine has its own standards of quality to maintain – but also its cost of advertising and promotion to cover; with something that is a 'house wine' of a reputable concern, the saving on the 'extras' can show in the price, but is not necessarily an indication that the wine is of lower quality. Try, too, to check on your own knowledge of the world's 'supreme sparkler' – there are many complexities, but also plenty of easy to understand booklets and books.

Theme: The variety of non-vintage Champagne – by establishment, by region.

Wines: If possible, have four wines: one from your regular source of local supply – such as have supplied the tastings in this book. All those mentioned have good 'B.O.B's, which means 'Buyer's own brand'. Waitrose have a very good one – but so have others. Then have one from an establishment in Rheims (or Reims if you're being French), another from one in Épernay and ideally one from Ay – between the two (see end note for some well-known names). If you can also put in a wine made entirely from white grapes (blanc de blancs), that's even more interesting and Marks & Spencer have a 'Blanc de Chardonnay', which is made solely from that great classic white grape alone, which is of impressive quality.

Practicalities: You'll know by now about cooling wines – an hour in the refrigerator or fifteen minutes in a bucket of ice and water. Don't forget the warnings about opening Champagne – never point the bottle at anyone or anything, never let go of that mushroom cork once you've removed the wire muzzle, let the cork come out with a discreet belch, not a vulgar pop, and direct the wine into nearby glasses instead of letting it foam wastefully over anything and everything.

In arranging the wines, sort out what comes from where. The label will tell you if you examine the small print. Put an ordinary non-vintage Champagne from Épernay first or early in the range, then one from Ay, then one from Rheims. With the wine (B.O.B.) from your local supplier, put this where the above applies, but, if it's a blanc de blancs, put it at the beginning. This doesn't have anything to do with the quality of the wines, only their weight – Épernay wines possess delicacy and lightness, generally making use of a lot of white grapes, Ay wines, in the middle of the region, are especially fine and elegant, Rheims wines are near to the greater vineyards culti-vating black grapes. The black grapes provide the fragrance and fruit, the white grapes the delicacy and finesse; a big blend, incorporating both, will then demonstrate the 'house style' of the establishment, veering to one sort of Champagne or another.

Tasting technique: Look at the colour – some non-vintage Champagnes are pale, light gold, others may have a hint of pink, like old Sheffield plate when it's getting worn. This shows the influence of the black grapes in the blend, lending their skin colour to the wine. A white wine made only from white grapes will be overall pale, possibly lemon-toned.

The smell: Unless it's frozen stiff, Champagne should have a delicious smell, light but definite, sometimes slightly flowery, sometimes almost piercingly fresh. Swing the wine round as with any still wine and sniff.

The flavour: In the past Champagnes were often very full, even sweet and fat. Today they are lighter in style – leaner in body one might say! – and although a B.O.B. will probably not be bone dry (which is no bad thing for general enjoyment), it certainly won't be sweetish. However, all will be individual –

some will have been deliberately made very slightly fuller and even sweeter than others, to please the drinkers. Note this, but try to differentiate between a wine that is rounded and a bit full (but not specifically sweet), and one that is fine-drawn and delicate. It's up to you to decide which you prefer, and on which particular occasions when you can enjoy Champagne.

Conclusion: Do you think it's worth paying the extra for certain Champagnes, or does this depend on the occasion? Which 'house Champagne' or B.O.B. pleases you for a party – or appeals most if you're having a bottle with a light meal, or creates the celebration atmosphere if you're offering it as an apéritif before a truly important meal?

If you are further interested, then you should try to plan a future tasting of, perhaps, some vintage Champagnes, or see whether the house wine you usually like is very different from a more expensive Champagne bearing a famous name. This is, after all, the sort of difference that exists, even though you may prefer the least expensive wine – but try to think out why you do so.

Should you really be able to splurge on a very special occasion, perhaps between close friends, try a couple of the luxury cuvées – Champagnes that represent the very finest that the producer can do. They will surprise you! Each will be completely individual! These, though, are not party wines – you need to enjoy them at leisure, with lightish food. If you want something original, try a pink Champagne or a comparison of two – for this you may have to go to a wine merchant, rather than a retail chain, but the light additional fruitiness is most interesting and means that you can have somewhat more flavourful food if you wish.

Suggested food: For a general party, a buffet can consist of several salads, plus more substantial fare. I suggest at least one fish pâté – possibly smoked mackerel or smoked salmon 'pieces' plus cod's roe, with a rather lightweight quiche, perhaps asparagus or spinach, or egg mousse. You could then have a chicken salad, or a turkey salad, or, if you haven't already had a lot of fish, a shrimp and rice and sweetcorn salad – but go easy on any piquant dressings and don't have too rich a mayonnaise. If you wish to offer a hot dish, veal in a cream and mushroom sauce or home-made chicken and ham rissoles or salmon fishcakes would be good. More simply, a really good fish or shellfish pie, perhaps with canapés of cream cheese and chives beforehand, would be nice 'blotting paper' – don't forget that Champagne pushes the alcohol along so that cosy fare is acceptable – or a platter of chicken drumsticks, slivers of loin of pork, a few twists of sausage, salami or, if you're lucky with your local butcher, 'boudin blanc' which is 'white pudding', with potato salad (use a little Champagne in the dressing while the potatoes are hot) and endive or lettuce will all be welcome. If you don't serve cheese, then sweet (but not chocolate) biscuits and meringues can accompany a fruit jelly and or/ices.

Some well-known Champagnes, divided according to where they are made:

Reims: Charles Heidsieck; Veuve Clicquot-Ponsardin; George Goulet; Heidsieck & Co. Monopole; Krug; Lanson; Louis Roederer; G. H. Mumm; Piper-Heidsieck; Pommery; Taittinger.

Épernay: Mercier; Moët et Chandon; Perrier-Jouët; Pol Roger.

Ay: Ayala; Bollinger; Deutz & Geldermann.

ENEMIES TO WINE

Quite a lot of fuss is made about 'what goes with what', but you'll have realised that, even within the cheaper ranges of wines, there's usually a selection that is suitable for most foods. There are a few things, however, that do make it difficult for you to taste the shades of flavour in a wine and, if you're trying to tackle a wine seriously, it's sensible to avoid anything that's likely to prevent you being able to get the benefit of the experience.

Smells

If there's a strong smell, even an agreeable one, in the room where you're drinking or tasting, this can fight with the smell of the wine. Maybe you do put flowers on the dinner table but, if you're tasting beforehand, perhaps it's wise to keep any strongly scented blooms out of the way. The same applies to cosmetics. Of course, *you* may not smell your scent, your hair spray or after-shave or the tobacco or cigars in your pocket, but anyone who is getting their senses trained to appraise wine can notice and find these smells a distraction. As for the strong smells of cleaning fluid, any aerosol 'fresheners', floor or furniture polish, a waft of even mouth-watering cooking from the kitchen, or the family pet who hasn't had a bath for far too long and lies under the table – these really do obtrude. Indeed, as you taste more and more, you'll find that there are more and more smells around. Of course, you can't banish all of them, but, if you're tackling wine even slightly seriously, try to do so in a fairly fresh atmosphere. It's just bad luck if someone's revving a car engine outside, or a neighbour has thrown a piece of rubber on a nearby bonfire, or there's been a spill of disinfectant in the house – or a guest arrives wearing an obviously costly but obtrusive perfume.

Flavours

What you start with – your own mouth – can obviously affect the way you taste. You already know how difficult it is to sniff the bouquet of a wine if your nose is bunged up with a cold. Well, if your mouth is still tingling from a minty toothpaste or an antiseptic gargle or mouthwash, it won't easily register any other tastes for at least a while. Nor, if you've just been sucking a boiled sweet, toffee or eaten a piece of chocolate will you find that the flavour of a wine gets through the taste already in your mouth. There are some smokers who say they can taste wine satisfactorily even when they've only just stubbed out a cigarette, but I rather doubt that, with the tobacco flavouring their mouth and affecting their saliva, they can taste neither wine or food with much discrimination. Does this sound severe? There are people who smoke while they're eating a meal – but I don't suppose they actually taste the food and they certainly spoil the enjoyment of those unfortunate enough to be near them. Could you appreciate the finest cooking if your neighbour were wielding a scent spray or some form of deodorant, fly spray or lavatory disinfectant?

There are not many foods that actually conflict with wines. You are not likely to want to select a wine to accompany curry, as its spicy hotness will overwhelm any drink. However, there are some things that swamp the taste of most wines, including very strong pickles, pepper, and hot mustard (the milder types won't be harmful in moderation) and, if you do have a food that is strongly flavoured with garlic or pungent herbs and if you like lots of vinegar on your salad, then a delicate wine won't really have much taste alongside. Eggs and eggy sauces can somehow coat the mouth, so that a light wine doesn't make much impression on the tastebuds. Citrus fruits, especially lemons, grapefruit and pineapple, which are pleasantly acid, can make some wines seem thin and bitter. You're not likely to be drinking very strong tea or black coffee just before a wine, but if you should do, you'll probably notice that the taste of these drinks, lingering in the mouth, can assert itself against the taste of the wine.

But even if you forget about possible palate changers, it's surprising how quickly you can get back to tasting seriously, even if you can't wash your mouth out with clean water. Don't, though, blame the wine for being 'off' or disappointing if there's any likelihood that it's your sense of smell and taste that are really at a disadvantage.

GLOSSARY

Abbocato/amabile This is Italian and means 'sweet' or 'slightly sweet'. Amabile is often used about Orvieto wines, which can be dry or sweetish.

Ampelography A word of Greek origin, meaning 'the study of grapes'.

Bin A wine bin is the series of racks or slots in which bottles of wine are kept – lying down, so that the cork is in contact with the wine and remains damp and swollen so as to prevent shrinkage and air getting in to the bottle. 'To bin' therefore means to arrange wines in the bin and, in the past, this was a skilled exercise, as one had to fit the wines into what might be awkward spaces in a cellar, with an uneven floor. A 'well set' bin should be so firm that someone can walk about on the top and so that a bottle can be pulled out of even the bottom row without disturbing the other bottles. For ordinary purposes, a carton in which wines have been delivered will serve as a bin, if tipped onto its side. Otherwise, plain wood and metal bins are practical and can be ordered (from most merchants) so as to fit even awkward spaces. Don't waste money on fancy wine bins or racks.

Blend This is a word that has somehow acquired unfortunate implications – but it doesn't deserve them. When you realise that the amount of wine from one single vinestock, yielding quite well, is approximately one litre and that this crop is harvested only once a year, you'll appreciate that this would be a mean ration for everyone wanting to drink wine! All wine is a blend of some kind: non-vintage wines, which make up the bulk of inexpensive wines, most Champagne, all 'house wines' are of course a blend, and assets of one vintage being combined with those of another vintage to make a better wine than would have otherwise been possible just from the wine of one year at a time. Then there are blends of grapes – Champagne is mostly a blend of black and white grapes, red Bordeaux is a blend of several black grapes, so are many of the finest wines of Spain and Portugal and so is Chianti. Different plots within an overall vineyard or, even, from one single estate all combine in the ultimate 'blend'. To make the cheaper wines of many regions, grapes from different areas, sometimes far apart, are blended into an harmonious wine. In the New World vineyards grapes and wine may come from vineyards hundreds of miles away from each other, all destined for blending. Indeed, the work of the blender is rightly referred to as an 'art', for it requies great skill and experience.

(What people perhaps mean, when referring to 'blended wine' is wines that bear the name of a famous vineyard or wine region with which other wines have wrongly been incorporated – this is the sort of thing that does make for wine 'scandals' but although it is naturally wrong to market, say, 'Chablis' that isn't Chablis at all, controls these days are pretty strict and penalties heavy for any infringement of legislation.)

Bottle stink The stale air that remains in the bottle of wine, just under the cork, can sometimes make the taster suppose that the wine is 'off' when the cork has just been drawn and the wine poured. If you wait even a few moments, this 'bottle stink' will disappear.

Boxbeutel/Bocksbeutel This is the squat, flagon-like bottle used for some wines. It was originally used only for the 'steinwein', a speciality of the Franconia region of Germany. Now there are various forms of it in use, although it is an awkward shape to 'bin'. The shape derives from the 'wineskin' in which wines used to be carried in medieval times.

Champagne method/Méthode Champenoise The process by which Champagne and the finer sparkling wines of the world are made. Because it's fairly lengthy and requires skill, these wines can never be really cheap.

Chaptalisation This process involves adding sugar to the 'must' (see pp. 178) so that the yeasts can work adequately during the fermentation process. It is in use, although subject to controls, in a number of the well-known vineyards, but it is perhaps best known in Burgundy which is both northern and, sometimes, cold. A properly chaptalised wine will remain 'in balance' and is rather like a pretty woman who has had discreet but adequate make up to go on looking pretty under artificial light. A badly chaptalised wine will tend to be 'soupy' and syrupy, out of harmony.

Co-op/Co-operative In a wine context, this refers to a group of growers who belong to an association enabling them to process and, perhaps, mature their wine in one place, and assist with marketing the wine. As machinery used at vintage time is lying idle for the rest of the year and as space in most small-scale farms and estates is limited for storage, this co-operative activity can be very helpful. In some regions the co-ops are very big and influential, with impeccable installations and the technical resources of highly-trained staff. Indeed, wines originating in a well-run co-op are not only likely to be good, they may possess considerable individuality, as members pool their 'know-how' and, with some of the famous co-ops, a tradition of dealing with certain buyers, including those in export markets, has been established so that the co-op will make ranges of wines likely to appeal to many different customers.

Cradle The wine cradle is used for bottles that have to be brought from lying on their sides in a bin or rack. Because there may be a deposit in the bottle, this is slid carefully out of the bin and, still on its side, placed gently in a cradle. Then the cork is drawn and the wine can be poured without the bottle standing upright – but, so as to avoid any churning up of the wine and mixing the deposit in it, the bottle should simply be progressively tilted over the glasses or into carafe, jug or decanter, so that there is no tilting up and down. Correctly used, the wine cradle is a piece of cellar equipment – but it should never be merely a means of serving wine at a table. You see how silly and indeed awkward it is to use the cradle, which takes up room on the table or sideboard and, unless all the wine is poured in one go, mixes up any deposit by the bottle tipping up and down over each glass. However, many chi-chi restaurants make use of the wine cradle – although ideally the wine waiter should only decant from it, alongside the table, if it has to be used. The cradle is said to be 'picturesque'. I don't think it's got any more right to be on a civilised dining-table than the chamber-pot has a right to be underneath! The place for the cradle – *if* it has to be used – is in the cellar and on the sideboard, not cluttering up the table and churning up the wine in the bottle.

Crystals These splinter-like glassy bits, that may be at the bottom of the bottle or attached to the cork, are tartrates and nothing to worry about, indeed, as they are the sign of a quality wine, rather the reverse. You can swallow them without risk.

Cuve/cuve close/cuvée The *cuve* is a vat and, therefore, the same word means the contents of that vat. Sparkling wines can be made by the *cuve close* or sealed vat method, which is also known as the *Méthode Charmat* after the man who perfected the process for commercialisation. The 'cuvée' is, more specifically, the 'vatting' or composition of the ultimate contents of the vat – i.e. blending. If you visit a wine estate in France, the 'cuverie' will be the vat house – that is, where the wine is made, the winery.

Demi-sec The term literally means 'half dry' but if you see it on the label of a sparkling wine, it will usually mean that the wine is rather sweet.

Doux French word, meaning 'sweet'. 'Dulce' and 'Dolce' are respectively Spanish and Italian words with the same meaning.

Elgin This is the curiously shaped glass, on a short stem, with a tallish, outward-curving bowl, often wrongly used for sherry. The 'schooner' is a larger version. It is supposed to have been named for the Lord Elgin who is famous for purchasing the marble statues from the Parthenon in Athens. The glass itself is horrible – it is quite useless to show off the smell or taste of any decent wine and no wine lover should accept it when it's possible to have a decent Paris goblet or tulip glass. (And the Elgin gives a mean measure – looking more than it is.)

Fermentation The process whereby grape juice becomes wine. It is complex and involves the action of yeasts. If you visit a winery at vintage time and see wine coming to birth, the experience will be wonderful – the bubbling of the 'must' while it is being transformed into wine is impressive. But never lean over any vat in which fermentation is taking place, because the gas being given off can upset your stomach.

Fiasco This is the Italian name for a 'flask', especially the raffia-bound plump bottle used for everyday quality Chianti.

It evolved from the wineskin used for transporting wine on one's saddlebow, but nowadays, even though the straw binding (which prevents bottles banging against each other) has often been replaced by plastic, it is difficult to find people to do the handwork. Good quality Chianti, anyway, is bottled in square-shouldered bottles that can be laid down for maturing.

Finish This is a wine talk term that means the final impression a wine leaves on the palate – does it trail away, does it snap off, does it give a favourable and pleasant taste right at the end, does it suddenly seem to fade away? Even a cheap wine should have a clean, agreeable 'finish' and some wines have a particularly delightful final taste.

Gay Lussac This term is the name of the man who, in France, evolved the system of measuring the strength of alcoholic beverages. This 'strength' is expressed as 'percentage of alcohol by volume', or 'Gay Lussac' and it is used world-wide, although some countries have other ways of measuring alcoholic strength. If you say 'percentage of alcohol by volume' or merely 'Gay Lussac', however, everyone will know what you mean and it is this that indicates the alcoholic strength of a wine on its label in the UK.

Green This is one of those pleasant terms that mean something wine lovers understand – though of course they don't mean that the wine concerned is green in colour! By 'green' is usually implied freshness, crispness, youth. But if a wine, such as a young Sancerre, doesn't seem 'green' to you, forget the term. (See Session 5 also)

Hock This is an English term used for Rhine wines, originating from the name of the town Hochheim. Although many people suppose it to have become current in Victorian times, in fact it seems to have been in use as early as the seventeenth century. But our ancestors also used the general term 'Rhenish' to refer to German wines overall.

Heurige This is the 'new' or recently made wine of the Vienna Woods, of which Grinzing is a well-known village, though there are others. From 11th November until the end of the year inns display a wreath or garland outside, to show they have the new wine, that can be drawn from the cask (thus perpetuating the 'bush' as in the English saying 'Good wine needs no bush'). It's chic and fun to go out to the Vienna Woods to drink the new wine, enjoy a snack and the singing of the musicians in the numerous taverns.

Jug wines Term used in the United States for wines of everyday quality.

Lagar Places where grapes are trodden in the port wine region.

Lage German word for a specific plot or site in a vineyard. Not to be confused with the 'grosslage' or overall vineyard, or the 'bereich', which is the overall general vineyard region.

Lees The lees are the residue or deposit of wine left in the cask after the main wine has been drawn off. But wine bottled 'sur lie' – as some Muscadet is – in other words 'off the lees' – will usually have a special tingling liveliness of style, which is much appreciated.

Legs/Tears/Gothic windows These are all terms for the trails that can often be seen forming down the sides of the bowl of a glass after you've swung the wine around. Their presence is usually the sign of a good wine. It need not be sweet.

Maderised/oxidised Terms used to describe wine that has suffered from being exposed to air. This can make white wines turn dark in hue, even becoming slightly brown. There is nothing harmful about a maderised wine, although it will not be at its best. To see what maderisation is like, leave a little wine in a glass, covered with a sheet of clean paper, and taste it after several hours, after a day, after two days and note the way in which either red or white wines change. Very old wines or wines that have been kept for too long in cask before being bottled can be like this. The process gets its name from association with Madeira – it can slightly resemble this fortified wine, but not always and only slightly.

Micro-climate If you haven't ever seen rain falling on one side of a road and the sun shining on another, you may find it difficult to believe exactly what difference a micro-climate can make! But, in wine regions, there can be even two or three micro-climates within the same village area, so that wines made from grapes grown in one plot will be different, some-times radically so, from those grown in the next door plot. The angle at which the sun strikes the vineyard, the channels of air, the warmth provided by distant but sheltering mountains or hills, can make a great difference.

Must This is grape juice before it has been transformed into wine by the process of fermentation. Most must is yellowish-green, rather like grapefruit juice, but a few grapes can tint it pink. If black grape skins are left in the must during the process of fermentation, the pigments on the skins will tinge the juice – and make red wine. In general, white wine is made from white grapes, red wine from black grapes or from a mixture of black and white grapes, but it's possible to make white wine from this mixture too – most non-vintage Champagne contains both black and white grapes. It's also possible to make a white wine from all black grapes – the skins are removed before they colour the must.

Noble rot This is called 'pourriture noble' in French. It is different from ordinary rot, which no grower wants to see developing in the vineyard. Noble rot is individual to certain areas, for example the Sauternes region of Bordeaux, the Rhine and Mosel in Germany. It is a type of fungus that forms on the ripe or overripe grapes, its action transforming the juice within them and, eventually, making very fine luscious wines. Because these wines are difficult to make they are never cheap (see 86–96).

Length A wine is said to possess 'length' if its finish (q.v.) is such that the impression it makes on the palate lingers and lasts for some time after it has been swallowed. Usually only fine wines possess much length, but there are French authorities who even time (in seconds) the length of certain wines, as they pass from the palate.

Organoleptic This is a term rather in vogue, but it merely means the different impressions made on the various senses involved in tasting a wine. Frankly, it's easier to say 'Taste impressions' and avoid being pompous!

Oenology The study or knowledge of wine. An oenologist in a wine firm is the person – man or woman – in charge of making and keeping the wine, very important.

Porrón The globular vessel, with a sharp-angled spout, in which many Spanish wines are served at table. This evolved from the wineskin of former times and drinkers would pass it from hand to hand, pouring the wine from the spout directly into their mouths so as to avoid mouth contact with the vessel itself. People wanting to show off in Spain sometimes pour the wine when holding the porrón high above their heads so that the stream of liquid flows down their nose, or from their forehead into their mouth, or they whisk the porrón about, twirling it, snatching at the wine as it curves from the spout. It's not very difficult to use the porrón in the basic way – but perhaps better to practise in the bathroom first.

Punt This is the hollow in the base of certain types of wine bottle, such as those used for claret and Burgundy. Originally, it was intended to act as a type of gutter and hold any deposit forming in the wine. Bottles with flat bases, such as those for German wines, were used for wines not throwing a deposit.

Pétillance A slight sparkle, sometimes only noticeable by the presence of tiny bubbles in the wine or, even, only perceptible by the tingling on the tongue when you drink the wine. Spritzig is the German term and some of the finest white wines have this touch of 'liveliness' when they are young. In many everyday wines, the pétillance is a pleasant asset.

Spumante Italian word, signifying a sparkling wine.

Stopper cork The type of cork that has a plastic or metal top, such as used in many sherries or other fortified wines. Stopper corks are practical, because, if rinsed in clean hot water, they can then be kept and used to stopper bottles of wines that are not all finished at a go; ordinary corks are sometimes difficult to re-insert into the bottle.

Sulphur Sulphur dioxide (SO_2) is possibly the most common form of disinfectant used in the world of wine. Ideally, there should be no trace of it in any wine that is ready for drinking, but sometimes if you visit a cellar or winery you may suddenly notice a 'catch' at your throat – and cough. This usually means that sulphur in some form has been used recently.

Ullage The space between the cork and the level of the wine. In an unopened bottle a lot of ullage could mean that the wine is not in prime condition.

Yeast There are many different members of what may be called the huge family of yeasts involved in making wine. Wine yeasts, however, are not the same yeasts as those used in baking bread or making beer, although they are similarly affected by temperature – if it becomes too hot or too cold they cease to do their work. Ideally, you should not notice any trace of yeast in wine, but sometimes, especially if the wine has very recently been bottled, there is a slight smell of it; anyone who has sniffed a bottle of yeast tablets will register this. Yeasts are the driving force behind all wine, transforming the must into wine.

GUIDE TO PRONOUNCING WINE NAMES

If you're ordering from a wine list, in a shop or a restaurant, you can always avoid trying to pronounce the name by simply giving the bin number, which will be alongside the particular wine. But why be shy? Even people behind shop counters or dignified-looking wine waiters don't always get the wine names right – the important thing is to get the wine you want and make it easy for someone to serve it or sell it to you. True, if you ask for 'Riceling' you may risk getting rice wine, and if you mix up the Sauvignon grape with the Savagnin or order Muscatel instead of Muscadet you may receive a surprise. So at least have a crack at the name.

With long words, split them up syllable by syllable and take them slowly. In the following list, stressed syllables are marked, otherwise each one has the same weight. Remember – there are nasty-looking long words in English too, especially some names – Cholmondeley, Marjoribanks, Cirencester. And what about all the different ways of pronouncing the 'ough' sound – cough, enough, bough, dough, plough? It doesn't matter if you go wrong, as long as the wine's the one you want. The sounds given here are what is usually described as 'southern English' – bear this in mind if you have a rich regional accent and modify it to vaguely BBC.

Wine Name	Approximate pronunciation
Aligoté	*Ally* gottay
Aloxe Corton	Aloss Corton
Alsace	Alzass
Anjou	On jew
Appellation Contrôlée	Appel *asion* Con*troh*lay
Armagnac	Ah man *nyac*
Asti spumante	*Ass* tee spoo*man*tay
Auslese	*Ows* layser
Barsac	*Baa* sack
Batailley	Bat eye ee
Bâtard-Montrachet	Bat ard Mon*rash*ay
Beaujolais	Boh zheo lay
Beaune	Bone
Beerenauslese	*Bee*ren ows layser
Bernkastel	*Bairn*kastel
Beychevelle	*Bay* chevelle
Blagny	Blan ye
Blanc de blancs	Blon de blon
Blanc fumé	Blon *fu*may
Blanquette de Limoux	Blonkette de Lee moo
Blaye	Blye
Boxbeutel	Box boy tell
Brouilly	Brew ye
Brut	Brute
Bual/Boal	Bwahl
Cabernet	*Cab* burn nay
Cahors	Ka oar
Champigny	Shom*peen* ye
Chardonnay	*Shah* donn ay
Chassagne-Montrachet	Shassanne Mon *rash*ay
Châteauneuf du Pape	Shat oh nerf do *Pap*
Chênas	*Shay* nass
Chianti	Key *ann* tee
Chinon	She non
Chiroubles	She *roubler*
Climens	Klee *monce*
Clos	Klo
Cos d'Estournel	*Koss* dess tour*nel*
Côte	Coat

Côte de Nuits/Côte d'Or/
   Côte Rôtie
	Coat de Nwee/Coat Door/
	   Coat Row tee

Coteaux	Cot oh
Cuve/cuve close	Coove/coove close
Cuvée	*Coove* ay
Daõ	Daow (through your nose!)
Douro	*Doo*roh
Echézeaux	*Ay* chez oh
Edelfäule	Ay dell foiler
Edelszwicker	Ay dels vicar
Eiswein	*Ice* vine
Estufa	Esh *too* fah
Filhot	*Fee* yoh
Fixin	Feesan
Gamay	Gam ay
Gevrey-Chambertin	*Jev*ree/*Sham*bertin
Gewürztraminer	Ger *vurts* traminer
Gigondas	Jig gon dass
Giscours	*Jeece* cor
Givry	*Jiv*ree
Graach	Grah ch (the last sound throaty as in 'loch')
Grand cru	Gron kroo
Haut Brion	Oh *bree*on
Hérault	*Ay*row
Hermitage	*Err*mitage
Heurige	*Hay*rigger
Hospices de Beaune	*Oss*peece de Bone
Jerez	Hay *reth*
Johannesburg	Yo *hann* iss burg
Juliénas	Yooly *ay* nass
Kabinett	Cabi*nett*
Lafite	La feet
Lage	La ger
Lascombes	Lass komb
Latour	Lattour
Lazio	Lahtzio
Mâcon	Mack on
Marc	Mar
Marche	Markay
Meursault	Mayr soh

Minho	*Mee*nyo
Moelleux	Mweller
Montilla	Mon*tee*yah
Montrachet	Mon *ra*shay
Montrose	Mon rose
Mosel/Moselle	Moh zell
Moulis	Moo leece
Mousseux	Moo sir
Mouton Cadet	Mooton *Kad*ay
Muscadet	*Muss*kadey
Nahe	Nah
Nierstein	Near stine
Nuits St. George	Nwee San Jorge
Oechsle	Erksler
Passe-tout-Grains	Pass too Gran
Pauillac	Poyack
Pedro Ximenez	Paydro Him*ay*neth
Pétrus	*Pay*trus
Pfalz	Pfalts
Phylloxera	Fill *ox* errah
Pichon-Longueville	Peeshon Longerville
Piesport	Peesport
Piesporter Goldtröpchen	Peesporter Gold *trurp* shen
Pinot	*Pee*noh
Pontet Canet	*Pon*tay *Can*nay
Pouilly Fuissé	*Pooy*ee *Fwee*ssay
Pouilly Fumé	*Pooy*ee *Foo*may
Pourriture noble	Poorittoor nobler
Puligny	Pooleenyee
Quincy	*Kan* see
Quinta	*Keen* tah
Rheingau	Rine gow
Rheinhessen	Rine *hess*in
Riesling	*Reece*ling
Rioja	Ree *och* ha
Roussillon	Roo see yonne
Rüdesheim	*Roo*deshime
Ruwer	*Roo*ver
Sancerre	Son sair
Sauternes	Soh tairn
Scheurebe	*Shoy* ray ber

Schloss Böckelheim	Schlos *Ber*kelhime
Sémillon	*Say* mee on
Sercial	*Sair* see al
Spätlese	*Schpayt* layser
Stein/steinwein	Shtine/shtinevine
Sur lie	Seur lee
Tafelwein	Tah fel vine
Tastevin	*Tass* ter van
Tokay	Too kye
Trockenbeerenauslese	Trocken beeren owslayser
Oerzig/Ürzig	Ertzig
Vacquéras	*Vack*ay rass
Valdepeñas	Val de *pain*yas
Valpolicella	Val pol ee *chel*lah
Venencia	Vain*nen* seeah
Verdelho	Vair *dell* yo
Verdicchio	Var*deeck*yoh
Vin blanc cassis	Vin blon *cass*eece
Vin de pays	Vin de pay
Vinho verde	Veenyo *vaird*
Vosne-Romanée	Vone *Ro* man ay
Waldrach	Valldrach
Wehlen	*Vay*len
Worms	*Voor*ms
Würzberg	Virtzberg
Yquem	Ee kem
Zeltingen	Zelltingen

THE NEXT STEP – LEARNING MORE
ABOUT TASTING

If you've enjoyed going through the tasting sessions, you may feel that you'd like to continue increasing your knowledge and appreciation of wine. How should you go about it?

First, try to learn a bit more about wine in general and the wines you've liked. There are plenty of first-rate paperbacks on sale, so the person who boasts that they 'haven't time' to get to know wine is really admitting that they haven't the energy or the inclination. You'll find some books listed on p. 2, although do remember that, in wine as in anything else, information can get out of date within a comparatively short time, so check the date when the book was published and when revised and updated.

Courses on wine

There are plenty of these, so that you can usually join a class. Of course, it may be expensive – usually, as with wine, you get what you pay for. Try to find a course, or single session, that you are going to *enjoy* as well as one that will really teach you something. Check with anyone who has done a similar course if possible. Take note of the qualifications of anybody who is going to lecture or teach: they may have high qualifications in the wine trade, they may have written books – are they the sort of speaker that will really help you and keep your attention in a session you attend after a day's work? Some who conduct 'tutored tastings' are respected tasters, but they are boring speakers. Some may be aiming what they say mainly at young students of the wine trade – is this going to appeal to you? It may be somewhat advanced and technical, it may be extremely dull. You might be better buying some more bottles and continuing your studies with friends! But if you sincerely want to learn, then you should try and find a lecturer or teacher who is going to provide more than an amusing talk accompanied by pleasant wines; this kind of thing is often done at dinners, but how much does it mean to you?

Going on tasting

If you've found the tasting sessions in this book helpful and enjoyable, then you can go on with similar sessions. But for this you must obviously extend the range of wines you try. Each one of the sources of supply that's mentioned will have a lot more wines all well worth sampling – experiment with these, always trying to look up whatever you try so that you find out something about it.

It's obviously also possible to do the 'mix and match' type of session – comparing the same wine from different growers or shippers – if you have access to different sources of supply. If possible, never restrict yourself to one single wine retailer. The 'house red' or 'dry white' of every single reputable merchant will be different and have something to contribute to your enjoyment.

Using different merchants

All the big retail chains will generally carry a range of most classic wines, so you have plenty of choice. But individual merchants will have the same – so explore them as well. Remember, whether the firm has been established in the seventeenth century or suddenly started within the past five years, there's no problem about your asking them to recommend a bottle for a specific purpose. Explain what you want and about how much you wish to pay – that's a challenge most merchants are delighted to accept. Their cheap wines ought all to be most interesting – they are the wines I buy for my own casual drinking – and they like to know the reactions of every interested customer.

Many of the big chains, such as those we've included here, have world-respected buyers obtaining their supplies, people who know the wines their customers like and who spare no efforts to get them, at an appropriate price. But, obviously, even with all the schemes for trade education, there can't be a qualified person alongside a supermarket shelf, nor can someone in a busy store, where beers, soft drinks, crisps and cigarettes are also being sold, always manage to give detailed advice and help to the wine-lover. This is where you will find it helpful to go to the merchant, who sells nothing else except wine, who loves it and who may know a lot about it.

Britain is unique in having more different outlets for wine than anywhere else in the world – so do profit by them! The independent merchants, who may often have several shops, may benefit by being able to buy wines available only in smaller quantities than the big chains require; they can provide services such as deliveries and often hold tastings for regular customers. Their lists are always worth study, for these contain notes on vintages, explanatory accounts of wine newly added to the list, plus particulars about additional services – hire of glasses, wine talks, discounts, recommendations on laying down and many more.

For the person wishing to specialise

Although, as has been said, most merchants will have stocks of the majority of classic wines, it's obviously impossible for even a huge firm to stock everything. Some of the most respected merchants may also be shippers and, as far as many are concerned, will have certain specialities for which they are famous and which anyone will find most interesting. For example, among the retailers mentioned here, Cullens have an extensive range of Chilean wines and are pretty good too on other wines from southern hemisphere vineyards.

At the other extreme, the historic London firm Corney & Barrow, who have an impressive list of classic wines, are particularly well-informed and stocked with an extensive range of different vintage ports from many of the major port houses and Cossart Gordon are likewise a wonderful source of old and special Madeiras, because the member of a great and old-established Madeira firm runs this side of the business. Remember that, with certain very fine wines that are always in short supply, the producer won't simply hand out the wines to the highest bidder – they are bestowed on firms whose prestige and standing is thought to deserve them and whose customers are likely to respect them.

Lists to study

In the following list, you will find a number of firms who are stockists of many fine classic wines – and if you see their names on restaurant lists, this indicates considerable respect. Averys of Bristol and O.W. Loeb of London are two merchants and shippers whose wines attract those who 'really know' and appreciate quality. I have indicated the specialities of such firms, but don't ignore their classic wines either.

But there are some firms who only stock certain wines, whose lists are equally worth study if you wish to pursue learning about, say, the wines of Spain, Portugal, Italy. You will learn a great deal from reading all these lists and, in the lists dealing only with certain wines, there may be much material that will enable you to set up a specialised tasting. Don't forget that, to the seriously interested, such firms are always willing to answer questions and help with advice on opening or even act as a point of reference if you have planned a special menu and wonder if the wine will go well with the food.

Behind every address, every telephone number there are human beings – they will be aware of your problems, social and financial, and be interested in your individual tastes. Don't hesitate to consult them.

Australia: Australian wines feature increasingly on lists, as study of supermarket shelves will have told you. Averys of Park Street, Bristol, have special knowledge of them and of New Zealand wines in addition to their long and magnificent list of classics and wines from every section of the world's vineyards.

Beaujolais: Roger Harris, Loke Farm, Weston Longville, Norfolk, stocks only Beaujolais – and every sort too. He specialises in the wines of individual growers and his fat list is informative and fascinating reading, virtually a general guide to Beaujolais.

California: These wines are also increasingly listed – when the exchange rate doesn't make them too costly! Geoffrey Roberts, Les Amis du Vins, 7 Ariel Way, London W12 and 51 Chiltern Street, London W1 has a long list, so does The Wine Studio, 9 Eccleston Street, SW1. Windrush Wines, The Barracks, Cecily Hill, Cirencester, Glos., GL7 2EF have California, Washington State, Oregon wines as well as classics.

England: Many English vineyards are now producing first-rate wines, often available at the vineyard or via local merchants in the south. You can also buy them – and the 'country wines' made from fruits, berries, flowers etc. – from Valley Wine Cellars, Drusilla's Corner, Alfriston, East Sussex; Merrydown Wine Co., Horam Manor, Horam Road, East Sussex; Mainly English, 14 Buckingham Palace Road, London SW1, and these places should usually also be able to provide a list of English vineyards open to visitors.

Italy: Many merchants have long lists of Italian wines these days, but some of the more specialised outlets include: Le Provençale, 167 Haverstock Hill, London NW3; Italian Wine Agencies, Wine Grower's Association, 230 Great Portland Street London W1 and their branches (mail order only); Stonehaven Wines, Grayshott Road, Headley Down, Bordon, Hants.; David Burns, High Street, Lymington, Hants.; John's Wines & Spirits, 131 Earl's Court Road, London SW3; Ashlyns-Trestini, 20 Chancel Street, London SE1.

Portugal: Grilli Wines, Little Knoxbridge, Cranbrooke Road, Staplehurst, Kent. For Madeira, Ellis Son & Vidler – see p. 190.

South Africa: Henry Collison, 7 Bury Street, St. James's, London SW1; Robert James, 79 Aslett St., London SW18; Cape Province Wine Importers, Clarence Road, Staines, Middx. Also Cullens, Averys of Bristol and Waitrose, Threshers and Ashe & Nephew.

Spain: The pioneers of Spanish wines from all regions and stressing fine quality in the UK were Laymont & Shaw, The Old Chapel, Millpool, Truro, Cornwall; others include Arriba Kettle, 5 St. Philip's Place, Birmingham; Scatchard's, 10–18 Victoria Street, Liverpool.; Pengallic Wines, 16 High Street, Thame, Oxon.; Wines of Spain, 4 Temple Court, Liverpool L2 6PY; Watson's, 2 Norfolk Place, Paddington, London W2.

Rhône and Loire: Yapp of Mere, Wilts. were the first to specialise in these wines and their list is imaginative and full of information and personal travel reminiscences. O. W. Loeb, 15 Jermyn Street, London, SW1, have the exclusivity for some of the finest Rhône wines of respected producers in addition to their classic list of French and German wines.

Recommended as well: Obviously it's impossible to cite all the good firms in the UK, but if you got the lists and asked for advice from the following you would benefit: Corney & Barrow, 12 Helmet Row, London EC1; Ellis Son & Vidler, 57 Cambridge Street, London SW1 and 27 White Rock, Hastings, Sussex; Lay & Wheeler, Culver Street, Colchester; Tanners, Wyle Cop, Shrewsbury; Adnams of Southwold; Laytons, 27 Midland Road, London NW1.

Other ways of buying

There has been a great vogue for buying wine via a 'club'. However, since retail price maintenance was abolished, this really is only useful as a means of getting a case or quantity discount by buying in bulk – usually three or five cases or more get a discount and this increases with the number of cases.

Mail order offers are subject to the same warnings: who is the firm and why has it got this 'amazing bargain'? If no details of shippers and sources of supply are given, you do need to be very sure of what you are doing if you are not to be landed with a quantity of mediocre wine.

Auctions? Again, you need to know what you're doing – and sometimes 'lots' are of several dozen, which you may not require. Sometimes, with cheap wines, it's possible to buy the same wine more cheaply from an ordinary merchant! For special wines, a merchant will always bid for you and you should anyway get an idea from the saleroom as to what sort of price a lot will reach.

Articles in newspapers and magazines: Here you can get to know what a variety of people find enjoyable and they will give prices and stockists, so that you will also become acquainted with the names of many merchants. If someone writing an article is a member of the wine trade, he ought to 'declare his interest', else he may, even without intending to do so, plug his wares. Otherwise, as with other interests, get to know the sort of writer whose advice you've found helpful and follow him.

For further reading and reference

So many books are published dealing with wine in general and special aspects of it that a long list might be compiled. The following are some that I've found helpful and practical, although for up to the minute information wine specialist magazines are possibly the best source of reference.

Alexis Lichine's *Encyclopedia of Wines & Spirits* (Cassell/ Christie's)
If you have to have one single book, this must be it! A huge and serious work of reference.

The Wine Book – Jancis Robinson (Fontana)
Stress is on the classic wines of Europe. Some of the retailers mentioned are now somewhat changed, but the advice on tasting, checking label information and the practicalities of handling and serving wine are sound.

The Penguin Wine Book – Pamela Vandyke Price
Tells you how wine progresses from grape to winery to bottle and the variations that may occur.

Specialist books:

The Wines of Bordeaux – Edmund Penning-Rowsell (Penguin)
Updated account of the regions and estates by an admitted authority. Not an easy read, but invaluable for the claret lover to refer to.

Burgundy – wines and vines – John Arlott & Christopher Fielden (Quartet)
Perhaps for the slightly advanced student, but essential and reliable.

Companion Guide to the Wines of Burgundy – Graham Chidgey (Century)
A basic account and practical guide to the region by a respected shipper.

Companion Guide to the Wines of Bordeaux ⎫ Pamela Vandyke
Companion Guide to the Wines of Champagne ⎭ Price (Century)
Written for the student and the traveller, these provide the
essentials on the wines plus practicalities for anyone visiting
the regions.

The Wines of Portugal ⎫
The Wines of Spain ⎭   Jan Read (Faber)
The history and the wines, region by region, with information
about the makers, by an established authority.

The Wines of the Rhône – John Livingstone – Learmonth &
Melvyn Master (Faber)
The wines and the makers described in detail.

Italian Wines – Victor Hazan (Penguin) and *Vino* – Burton
Anderson (Little Brown) deal in two different ways with the
complex subject.

The German Wine Atlas (Davis Poynter) provides maps and
much guide information for the visitor, as well as essentials on
German Wine Law and the vineyards.

The World Atlas of Wine – Hugh Johnson (Mitchell Beazley)
This has detailed maps of the regions, plus a brief commentary
and elegant diagrams and pictures. It is frequently updated.

Wine Tasting – Michael Broadbent, M. W. (Christie's)
This gives the world-famous professional's approach to the
subject of tasting of the finest wines.

Enjoying Wine – Pamela Vandyke Price (Heinemann)
Written for the ordinary person – but the sections dealing
with the senses involved and the physiology may, because in
layman's language, help anyone who wants to go further in
this exercise.

Books on the wines of California, South Africa, Australia, New
Zealand are now available fairly easily, but some care should
be observed in relying too heavily on the multitude of small-
scale guides to wines, as these may be out of date within a year
or two of publication and, being written in 'telegraphese', they
can be somewhat unhelpful to the inexperienced.